CONSUMPTIONOMICS

Asia's role in reshaping
capitalism and saving
the planet

CONSUMPTIONOMICS

Asia's role in reshaping capitalism and saving the planet

Chandran Nair

John Wiley & Sons (Asia) Pte Ltd

First Published in 2011 by
Infinite Ideas Limited, 36 St Giles Oxford, OX1 3LD, United Kingdom

Other Wiley Editorial Offices

John Wiley & Sons, 111 River Street, Hoboken, NJ 07030, USA
John Wiley & Sons, The Atrium, Southern Gate, Chichester, West Sussex, P019 8SQ,
        United Kingdom
John Wiley & Sons (Canada) Ltd., 5353 Dundas Street West, Suite 400, Toronto, Ontario,
        M9B 6HB, Canada
John Wiley & Sons Australia Ltd., 42 McDougall Street, Milton, Queensland 4064,
        Australia
Wiley-VCH, Boschstrasse 12, D-69469 Weinheim, Germany

Library of Congress Cataloging-in-Publication Data
ISBN 978-0-470-82857-1

Typeset in 11/14 Sabon Roman by Cylinder
Cover design by Karl Anders
Printed in Singapore by Toppan Security Printing Pte. Ltd.
10 9 8 7 6 5 4 3 2

To Sumathi Letchimy Narayanan and Kadangot Parameswaran Nair

CONTENTS

'[World] population is projected to rise from 6.7 billion to 9 billion between now and 2050, and more and more of those people will want to live like Americans.' [1]
Thomas L. Friedman

PREFACE

Some twenty years ago, I found myself speaking more and more at a range of business and other forums on what I loosely called environmental issues. A recurring theme was the links between these issues and a range of social, economic and political challenges. Over time, I became increasingly preoccupied by what would happen if Asia continued to develop along Western lines – in particular, if countries across this huge and disparate region were to adopt consumption-driven capitalism as both their goal and their means of reaching that goal.

Often I found myself tempering my opinions, worried I would be accused of being unqualified or poorly informed on many of the issues I addressed. But as the speaking opportunities continued to arrive, I found myself testing more of my half-baked ideas to see how they were received.

I discovered that some parts of my audiences, notably business leaders and policy makers, often looked uncomfortable with my suggestion that the current trajectory was unsustainable. But there were others who were broadly receptive, even if the more supportive comments were often made privately after a meeting had ended.

I was curious. Who were the Brahmins deciding what topics were acceptable, which views could be expressed? Could I speak out more?

Certainly, the opportunities to do so increased, as more and more forums began including an obligatory session – sometimes an entire event – on topics familiar to me, the ones I had spent years working on as a

CEO and environmental consultant managing projects across Asia, from China and India to Indonesia, Thailand and Vietnam.

Despite sparing no effort to avoid offence by being as polite and courteous as possible, I often found myself accused of being unwarrantedly negative and pessimistic – the last a charge I found difficult to accept, having long regarded myself as an incorrigible optimist.

At one forum in Sweden, a senior United Nations official told me, albeit in a friendly manner, that I was a 'demagogue'. I sensed that while he agreed with much of what I said, like many UN officials, he was worried that I had breached some unspoken protocol by throwing out a challenge to the business leaders, politicians, academics and others in the audience.

At another meeting, a regional economic summit in Hong Kong in the mid 1990s, I was clearly the token 'environmentalist'. I spoke about the dramatic deterioration of air quality in the Greater Pearl River Delta region, and questioned the conventional view that investment and growth would lead to a prosperity that, in turn and more or less automatically, would create the conditions for the environment to improve. I was told that my concerns about the environment were laudable but my fears were overblown; I should not worry as it would never get that bad, and before it did, business would respond.

Fifteen years on, the pollution in Hong Kong and its neighbour, Guangdong, has worsened, and conference themes have expanded in scope – from how to be a better environmental citizen and green your operations to addressing global climate change and sustainability.

A talk in the United States in 2008 drew a different response. Even though the audience was a largely liberal crowd – more Oprah/Obama than Sarah Palin/Tea Party – my suggestion that if Americans were serious about global warming then they might think about taking some action at home was not well received. Clearly, even floating the idea that consumption could be tempered – perhaps by restricting car ownership to one vehicle per household, introducing a carbon tax or possibly even eating less – was tantamount to foreign interference in US internal affairs.

Nonetheless, as climate change moved up the political agenda and into the mainstream, I found myself encountering less direct rejection of what I had to say. The calls for corporate social responsibility increased, and more and more forums made room for inspirational speakers calling on their audiences to become more responsible eco-citizens and 'be the change' (watch the TED talks). Leadership remained in, but only if it took note of new social networks that were mobilizing citizens to take action. 'Sustainable' solutions replaced innovative ones, consumers became ethical, and companies were urged to reduce their environmental footprints because going green meant saving money – simultaneously benefiting the world, their customers, themselves and their shareholders.

At least, however, the issues were being raised. And slowly – far too slowly – attitudes began to alter. In June 2009, speaking in Bali to a group of clients of one of the world's oldest private wealth banks, I outlined the conundrum that consumption-led growth posed for Asia. I was surprised at the level of interest I generated. Several even accepted my throwaway lines that 'bling is out', 'less is more' and that constraints had to be put on consumption. In the audience was the CEO of a leading global publisher. I had expected to be dining alone, but instead I ended up hearing him suggest that I should expand and write down what I was saying. What you are reading is the result of our conversation.

Neither East nor West

The form of this book took a while to emerge. At its heart lies a discussion about the re-emergence of Asia as an economic power, and the dilemma this poses to itself and the world. But as I shared tentative outlines with a few friends, I was often told to make sure what I said could not be attacked or dismissed as an anti-West rant.

These warnings troubled me. Why was it that these people liked the idea of having me air my views, but believed they should warn me about the likely reaction from the elite inhabitants of the well of conventional wisdom? Would it really be so dangerous to draw attention to what was clearly visible not just to me but to any reasonable being? After all, every day of the week it is possible to find articles and op-ed pieces in the international press critical of China and India, and it would not take long to find other articles criticizing the way in which every other country in the region is run.

Anyway, to clarify matters, this book is far from being an attack on the West. It is not about how the West has got things wrong. Nor is it about how Asia will get them right. It is certainly not about this being the time for Asian ascendancy and how the West will now have to understand the new rules. There is a growing band of commentators, including many Asians, subscribing to these kinds of arguments – ones which I believe are dangerous.

As far as it attacks anything, it is the path Asia is taking, and the unquestioning nature of the decision to go down this path taken by its leaders in the face of mounting evidence that doing so can only hurt their countries, not help them.

This book does, however, advocate new rules. And it is not saying that the West is without responsibilities. Many people in Europe and America have taken their governments to task for not matching their rhetoric with actions, be it over development aid, climate change or military action around the world. It is vital that pressure continues to be maintained on these and other issues – however unlikely it may appear that results will be forthcoming. But what the West should do is not my subject. Rather, this book addresses the question of what Asian societies must do – most importantly, what their governments must do.

As it became ever clearer to me that the direction Asia was taking had to change, I increasingly wondered why it was that so many Asian business leaders, many of whom had studied at what were commonly acknowledged to be the world's best universities and business schools, so rarely addressed these issues of resource depletion, environmental degradation and backward governance. Why the silence? Were they so busy they had no time to think about them? Or were they convinced that really there was no problem: the costs would be short term, and beyond that prosperity would eventually trickle down?

I began to wonder if they were just too scared to speak out, worried about what their companies or business partners might say. The more I got to know some of them and listened to their ever more frequent 'green speeches', the more I became convinced that, despite their power, they were too afraid to be more intellectually robust, except in private. For most of them, I suspect, the reason was simply not wanting to step out of line – after all, the system, whatever its contradictions, had rewarded them. Why question the Harvard Business School model of supply-chain management – a convenient way of shifting unwanted external factors, such as pollution, to developing countries – if they could rise to that ultimate point of professional recognition as the Asian representative on a multinational's board?

Other factors were also at play. More and more I noticed the ways in which the elite business schools of the world, most of them American, were shaping the thinking of their Asian students. It seemed to me that these young minds – some of the brightest in the region – were going to these schools not to be taught practical skills that would make them better, more responsible citizens, able to help the problems of their home countries, but rather to be schooled in an ideology.

Learning how to manage and innovate within the limits and constraints imposed by our planet featured nowhere in their teaching. Instead they were told how, via its reliance on free markets, capitalism had emerged as the best means of creating prosperity. Governments had a role in all this, but principally to remove obstacles such as unnecessary regulations. Throw in democracy as the icing on the cake, and not only had the West succeeded in advancing civilisation to new heights of well-being and scientific achievement, but it had also, as Francis Fukuyama observed, arrived at the end of history.

Such hubris, of course, almost inevitably precedes a fall. But even now I am still startled at just how self-assured this view of this world was, and how much it remains intact. I teach a course at an MBA School, and continue to marvel at how little its students – many of them Asian, but also from America and Europe, and almost without exception Western-educated – feel any need to question the assumptions on which they will base their careers and lives. Even today, despite the economic success of their home countries, most of them continue to play down their origins, preferring instead to aim for a high-flying career at an investment bank or multinational. They are smart, very smart, but intellectually neutered.

Governance

In considering the disparate but interlocked issues of silence and denial, I began to wonder about their possible connection with one other issue that was troubling me: why it was that the need for us to organize ourselves to live sustainably – fairly, equitably, and within constraints – had not kept pace with our ability to innovate technologically.

Through the twentieth century, at an ever-accelerating rate, humanity proved able to increase its power over nature in the most extraordinary ways. Where we failed, however – and failed abysmally – was in our ability to govern our innovations. Our inventions sped ahead, but our ability to monitor and regulate their impact lagged dangerously behind. Typically action was taken only when something went badly wrong, as is happening in the wake of BP's disastrous Gulf of Mexico oil spill. We have not found the means to integrate our technological and financial innovations with the need for limits and rules, where necessary draconian, to impose restraint on how we live.

The evolving role of technology also provided the ingredients for yet another headache. Today, more than 2.2 billion people in Asia have access to mobile phones – far more than have access to potable water or sanitary toilets. I first noticed this gap between the availability of technology and that of basic necessities when I worked in Bangkok in the late 1980s. Friends who lived on the banks of the Chao Phraya River had televisions and video players, but they used the river as a sewer and its polluted waters for washing. Since then, even slum dwellers have migrated to mobile phones and iPods, but their refuse still pours untreated into the river. Similar sights can be seen across Asia, in Delhi, Jakarta and Manila.

But how is it that, while mobile phones and other electrical goods have become ever cheaper, lavatories are still a luxury item? Why is it that the best minds are helping companies make more iToys or banks rework their balance sheets, not shaping the governance that will determine our collective future? This book explores my answers to these questions – that we live in a world whose values are set by an economic system that incentivizes and rewards those who can generate growth for a select group of mostly Western institutions.

New values

To pre-empt suggestions that I am trying to revive the Asian values debate of the 1990s, nowhere in this book do I suggest that Asia will get it right because it has governments or cultures more suited to coping with the challenges of the twenty-first century than other parts of the world. This book does, however, argue that because of its sheer weight of numbers Asia faces an imperative to get things right that is less intense in other parts of the world. Thus it is about Asia's responsibilities and obligations at this particular point in history.

It seeks to contribute to the narrative about these issues in the region and therefore in the world too. I take seriously the fact that global debates are – alas – dominated by Western commentators, politicians and business leaders. Asian perspectives are badly needed (as are those of Latin America, the Middle East and Africa).

It is both a challenge and an appeal to capitalism. One of capitalism's strengths is its ability to adapt to new realities. And Asia is perhaps now, given its stage of development and the harsh realities it faces, most suited to freeing capitalism from being the captive it has become of free market fundamentalists and ideologues.

This is not a book about climate change. Nor is it a doomsday book. But it is a book about the catastrophes – some of which are already upon us, and many more that lie ahead – if the world, and particularly Asia, continues on its current trajectory. Most of these will be of a creeping, insidious nature – those of people struggling to survive in depleted or disaster-struck environments, or being forced to give up farming and migrate to cities because they can no longer grow enough produce to feed themselves, or having to watch the forests they and their families have lived in and depended on for generations be felled and replaced with palm-oil plantations so we can all have cheap cookies.

Possibly, further off into the future, worse fates may be in store for us. But my goal is not to spread fear by predicting dire outcomes. Rather, this book is a call for us to abandon the goal of realizing consumption-driven capitalism across Asia, and replace it with a different objective – of having an environment that we can pass on to future generations, one with rainforests, with biodiversity, with adequate resources, both renewable and non-renewable; one that is not poisoned, that has fish in its oceans; one with cities that are a pleasure to live in; and, of course, one with a climate that is not running out of control. This book will, I hope, make readers understand that without dramatic changes in our levels of consumption, the challenge of climate change cannot be meaningfully addressed.

Of course, climate change plays a big role in this book, but at its heart is a call to embrace sustainable ways of living. As such, this is a book about realizing change, primarily in Asia – and possibly beyond. Doing so calls for questioning and redefining many ideas and concepts. The financial crisis prompted many in the West to suggest that it was time to question many of the core ideas that had guided countries through the last few decades. Asians must do the same.

Rejection will be an important part of this – a critical first step. But rejection alone is not enough. We need to rethink policies, and political action, about how we define growth, wealth creation, what we can do and own, and how we should work and live. We must question the assumption that everyone in Asia should aspire to own a car, live and work in air-conditioned surroundings, and consume food and goods shipped from every corner of the world. But we must do all this in order to come up with something new. Doing this on the scale called for is a political task. The changes that will be necessary will require political action to determine their precise direction, to gain support and to overcome resistance. As I discuss further in the final chapter, this means that at its heart this is a political book, one about how people decide the rules under which they and others in their societies should live.

No silver bullets

When seeking feedback on my ideas, I was often told that stating problems without offering any suggestions for solutions would leave readers short-changed. I have borne this in mind, and this book contains proposals that I think governments could usefully follow. However, it contains no silver bullets. It refuses to take refuge in hopes that technology and finance, encouraged by markets, can see us through. If only it was that easy. But as well as asking questions, it looks for ways forward, attempting to move beyond feel-good solutions to identify some of the far harder decisions that will have to be taken.

Many of these decisions can only be taken if we first accept that change will not all be win-win. Yes, there will be winners – but there will also be losers, most prominently some of those who have benefited most from the current institutional set-up. Tackling such vested interests will require willpower and – the biggest anathema of free market ideologues – strong states.

As much of what people have bought into will need to be deconstructed if we are to live as many on a crowded planet, a strong and independent media would also be useful, as would robust civil societies. But if I were to prioritize one of these, it would be the force to devise and enforce the laws and regulations that our societies need. Consequently, this book is addressed above all to government officials and policy makers. These are the people who will have to draw up the agendas, build support and implement change.

Policy success, however, will only come if it receives broad public backing. For this reason, I have striven to produce a book that is accessible to as broad an audience as possible. Among this number, I hope, are many business people – some of whom, perhaps, are genuinely willing to take seriously such often-repeated mantras as 'creative destruction', 'innovation', 'change agents' and 'risk'. Harnessed properly, these could be forces that rework how people live. Almost all companies talk about the need to 'think outside the box'. I hope the next few decades will show us that they can.

Definitions

It is in the nature of a book such as this to be reliant on sweeping generalizations. I apologise for this, while hoping that critics, before picking on the inevitable weaknesses or contradictions they are sure to find, first ask whether there is a greater question that it is better worth their time addressing.

By Asia I mean the countries of east, south-east and south Asia. Australia and New Zealand are excluded, as are the central Asian states. Usually, but not always, I include Japan; I leave it up to the reader to decide when doing so is inappropriate. I refer often to the countries I discuss as developing nations, ignoring the fact that the wealthier parts of east Asia have more in common with Europe or even America than, say, with Myanmar or Afghanistan.

In using the term 'Asia' I am conscious that many will question whether it is simply too big and diverse a collection of countries to be treated as a single entity – or, worse still, accuse me of adopting a Western reductionist construct for what are a hugely disparate group of countries. These are valid criticisms, but not ones I feel any great need to address in any depth. My reasons for this are twofold. First is that this book is not focused on a geographical cluster of nations, but on ones that for a host of reasons are home to a huge number of people living in economies that in recent years have realized sustained periods of economic growth. Thus, it is this part of the world that has the greatest potential to impose stress on our planet if it decides to opt for a consumption-driven model of growth. Second, it is a region that despite its political, cultural and social differences is increasingly being pushed closer together; many of its environmental challenges are cross-border. Combined, these two reasons make it a part of the world with great responsibility for finding new ways to navigate through what remains of the twenty-first century.

More often than not, my discussions relate to the region's two giants,

China and India. Because of their scale, decisions and actions in these countries will affect the world in ways that those taken in most others will not. But other countries have vital roles. The fate of Indonesia's rain forests is one of the pivotal issues facing the region; as is what happens in the Coral Triangle, a sea area of 2.3 million square miles embracing the Philippines, the eastern parts of Malaysia and Indonesia, the coast of northern Papua New Guinea and the Solomon Islands, nine-tenths of which is threatened by over-fishing, particularly that using explosives.[2]

And no country will escape the impact of environmental change. Pakistan was already one of the world's most environmentally overstressed countries before devastating floods swept through it in 2010. Bangladesh will have more people affected by rising sea levels than anywhere else worldwide. In east Asia, Japan, South Korea and Taiwan may already have the wealth that allows them to look at environmental threats through developed-world lenses, but none will be able to escape the devastation that will follow if conflict over resources were to spill over into war.

As for other parts of the world, I use the phrases 'the developed countries' or 'the rich countries' as shorthand for the nations of North America and Western Europe. Japan is sometimes included in this number, sometimes not. The United States features as the representative figure of the 'West', itself a word I use throughout this book, often imprecisely, but which I feel conveys that body of ideas embracing freedom and power that so many in Asia find both alluring and disturbing.

Finally, Africa merits a brief note. I cannot claim to understand that vast continent, but having lived and worked there, I think I can say that the issues raised by this book have the utmost relevance to its countries. The timescale may be slightly different, but the questions people there will have to face will be the same as those now being raised in China, India and other Asian countries – whether adopting the Western consumption-driven model of growth can in any way aid their development, or whether it will have precisely the same impact as in

Asia, eroding the possibilities of a flourishing future. Asians cannot have it all, and nor can the people of Africa.

Hong Kong, September 2010

Population
Billions

Real GDP
Trillion dollars*

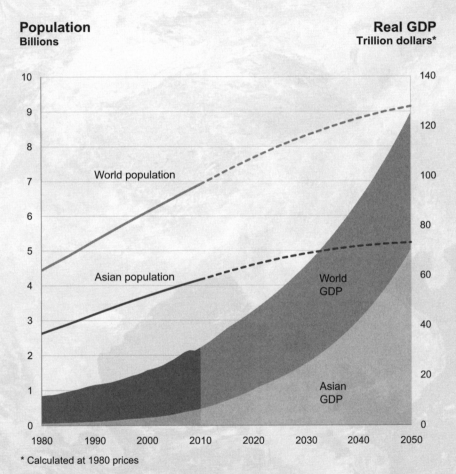

* Calculated at 1980 prices

Source: Population, United Nations; GDP, International Monetary Fund (1980-2015),
Global Institute for Tomorrow (2016-50)

INTRODUCTION – IN DENIAL

As the global financial crisis played out through 2008 and 2009, I was repeatedly struck by the bizarre disconnect of economists and policy makers. Amidst collapsing financial markets and talk of another great depression, there were repeated calls for consumers – especially in Asia, and above all China – to drive global growth by consuming more.

Much of this was framed in terms of 'rebalancing' – that what the world needed was for heavily indebted Westerners, especially Americans, to take their feet off the consumption pedal, while Asians did the reverse, spending more and saving less. It was an appeal much of Asia bought into, and why not? Finally, after two centuries of living in the West's shadow, Asia's re-emergence as the mainstay of the world economy looked imminent.

In India and elsewhere across the region, government leaders privately gloated as Western governments nationalized banks and insurance companies, and GM and Chrysler were sent running into the arms of the US government. After years of being lectured on the need to open their markets, privatize state assets and allow their currencies to float freely, theirs were the economies that had withstood the financial meltdown.

Chinese officials in particular enjoyed what looked like vindication of their country's model of state-managed capitalism, as their economy, albeit helped by a massive stimulus package, kept steaming ahead. From around the world, plaudits arrived – Barack Obama's among them – praising China for its achievements, but also asking it to do more. Then the world's third biggest economy, and now the second largest, could it become the new driver of global growth? In particular, could its people be persuaded to become the world's new big spenders?

China's leaders appeared willing to engineer this new role. The country's premier, Wen Jiabao, speaking at the 2009 Davos summer forum held in Dalian, a city on China's north-eastern coast, announced 'We have made vigorous efforts to stimulate consumption and make domestic demand, particularly consumer spending the primary driver of economic growth.'[1]

Shortly after, Anoop Singh, the director of the International Monetary Fund's Asia and Pacific Department, echoed Wen's line: 'The mainland consumer has been held back for too long, and now must be put front and centre in China's growth model.' Ensuring the best way of doing this, he continued, had been the subject of a special IMF workshop in Beijing that had brought together Chinese officials, academics, international analysts and IMF staff to discuss 'how best to catalyse household consumption in mainland China'.[2]

Roughly concurrent with these events, governments around the world were preparing themselves for the United Nations' climate change summit to be held in Copenhagen. For sure, sceptics continued looking for holes in the scientific explanations that underpinned our understanding of what was happening to the world's climate. But, finally, it seemed, the world was about to get serious about its biggest single environmental threat after years of foot-dragging.

But here was the disconnect: if the underlying cause of climate change is the consumption-fuelled growth that has driven the world economy – particularly in the last few decades – then why would anyone be advocating more of it?

Disconnected

Of course, we now know that the Copenhagen summit ended in failure and acrimony. The consequences of that are impossible to foresee, but in mid-2010, as the final parts of this book were being drafted, Pakistan was witnessing its worst-ever floods, China was recovering from huge floods in its south and Russia was reeling from forest fires whose severity stemmed from a heat-wave and its worst drought in decades. Climate change, though not directly responsible for any of these events, has exacerbated them. Their pattern, combined with record high temperatures elsewhere around the world, highlights the trend of ever more extreme weather that climatologists have widely forecast.

While we do not know in detail what will happen, we already know many of the costs of what will happen. The World Bank, for example, forecasts that developing countries will need to spend a total of between $40 to $100 billion every year from now until 2050 on adapting to the effects of climate change on their farming sectors.

Moreover, no one denies that climate change is only one of a host of environmental and resource challenges the world faces. One after another, the world's great fisheries are being depleted to the point of no return. Tropical rain forest continues to be felled to feed demand for hardwoods. The excessive use of chemicals in farming is poisoning land. 'When the word "water" appears in print these days, crisis is rarely far behind,' John Grimond noted in *The Economist* in a special report on water published in May 2010.[3] The same is true of food. Droughts and rising oil prices sent food prices soaring in 2007–08, leading to unrest and riots around the world. Spiking grain prices in 2010, also caused by droughts, had UN and other officials worrying about a rerun.

Wherever we look we see ecological and environmental crises caused by human activity. But, paradoxically, while we are increasingly certain about the long-term effect our actions are having on the world, if not in detail then certainly in their broad impact, we refuse to tackle their root cause: the way in which we treat the natural resources the world has given us.

The world is in a massive state of denial. The problems we must deal with are transparently clear, but we refuse to take action. Instead, people hope that something will turn up. A magical rebalancing system in earth's nature? Some technological fix that will allow us to create clean energy from renewable sources or pump carbon dioxide into the belly of the planet? Management systems that allow us to clean up as we go along? A way of harnessing our self-interest via free markets that will encourage businesses to produce 'green' goods that simultaneously satisfy our ever-expanding desire to consume more but have negligible environmental effects?

All these have been suggested. The American Nobel-winning physicist Robert Millikan famously pronounced in 1930 that the earth was just too big for humanity to damage it. As the environmental historian J.R. McNeill points out, that was the year in which chlorofluorocarbons, chemicals which destroy the ozone layer, were invented.[4] The Danish writer and professor Bjørn Lomborg continues to suggest that the best thing we can do is forget about trying to cut carbon emissions now and instead spend money on technology research and development into non-carbon energy sources.[5] BP, long before its disastrous spilling of oil into the Mexican Gulf, had been trying to persuade the world that it had the answer to our needs through a re-branding campaign centred on the tagline 'beyond petroleum'.

This inability to join the dots linking the way we run our economies to the effect that doing so has on the world is bizarre. How is it that intelligent, capable people – such as Anoop Singh and his colleagues in Beijing – can so confidently call for stepped-up consumption to be China's priority?

The answer is not so hard to find. It lies in the free market ideology that secured global hegemony in the last three decades – nowadays known as market fundamentalism – and its astonishing claim to be the answer to almost everything. The British thinker John Gray highlights the nature of these claims during its golden era of the 1990s:

Those were the years when slackers throughout the world were enjoined to submit themselves to the rigours of 'the Washington consensus' – a mix of dogmatic policy prescriptions and hypocritical rhetoric that enjoyed the support of the great majority of economists. According to that consensus, the market regime that was installed in Britain, the US and a few other countries from the 1980s onwards could not only ensure stability and promote steady growth there but was a model – the only possible model – for countries everywhere. The one truly rational economic regime, free market capitalism, was also the most productive. As such it was bound to drive every other system out of existence, and would eventually be adopted worldwide. This faith in the universal spread of free markets animated much of the thinking of the American-led institutions overseeing the world economy, such as the IMF. Along with economists in university departments in much of the world, these institutions succumbed to a quasi-religious belief that the free market was the germ of a single, universal economic system.[6]

There was – and still is – some truth in market fundamentalism's claims to efficacy. Freeing up markets can be an effective way of ensuring economic growth. They helped the United States and Europe, particularly the United Kingdom, escape the clutches of stagflation that bedevilled the late 1970s. In the decades that followed, other countries that adopted similar prescriptions of open markets and light government appeared to prosper – China, of course, where more than 300 million people have been lifted from poverty in the last thirty years, and more recently India, where the growth rate rose sharply once it began freeing its markets. For sure, there were problems along the way – the Asian financial crisis, the collapse of Long Term Capital Management and the dotcom bubble, to name but three – but overall economic growth remained strong, with the world economy growing by around 50 percent in total size between 1990 and 2008.[7]

Although 'market fundamentalism' principally took root in the English-speaking world – the United States, of course, but also in the United Kingdom, New Zealand and Australia – its discourse and practices took hold in every corner of the world, further promoting the idea of 'globalization' as being an unstoppable force.

Some countries, such as Japan and Germany, were less receptive to these ideas. But even in these places there was a general acceptance of 'Washington consensus' notions as being the best ones for promoting economic efficiency, via having more flexible workforces, more open markets and more exposure to global competition. China kept various key sectors off-limits to foreign business, but lowered its barriers to trade and investment in many industries, and allowed the creation of a low-paid, largely docile workforce for the export-oriented factories that sprung up along its eastern coast. India, after years of being mocked for not opening its doors to Western multinationals, followed in its wake, deregulating trade and investment, lowering taxes and privatizing parts of the public sector, but maintaining agricultural subsidies and making little change to its labour laws.

Vigorously promoted by other Western institutions, such as the World Trade Organization, World Bank and International Monetary Fund, and their local counterparts such as the Asian Development Bank, these theories became the norm – perhaps even more so in Asia than any other region outside North America. By the mid-1990s, with south-east Asia in its boom era, China attracting its first massive wave of foreign investment and India having ended its experiment with socialist economic management in favour of market liberalization, they were dominant. The only places that resisted them were the ostracized regimes of North Korea and Myanmar, and a few other forgotten corners such as Bhutan.

Around the world, crises came and went. Mexico's tequila crisis, the Asian financial crisis, Russia's default and the ensuing collapse of Long Term Capital Management, and then the dotcom collapse were all seen off. With Alan Greenspan running the US Federal Reserve, manipulating interest rates to keep growth coming, many started to believe the American economy, and with it the world's, had entered a new era where the business cycle and recessions had been relegated to history.

The problems markets could not solve were largely brushed aside. Notions such as equitable distributions of wealth were replaced with such ideas as trickle-down economics – that helping businesses or the rich via tax cuts would stimulate the economy and so benefit everyone. And what was true within economies also held between them. Lowering obstacles to cross-border investment and the trade in goods would lead to companies creating jobs, transferring technology and making more of the goods that local consumers wanted at prices they could afford.

As the global economy boomed, business basked in success. And from this it was an easy step to suggest that what was good for business, was good for growth, and so must be good for a country. Markets, growth and companies thus became the interlinked solution to all problems – one that was not only seen as the best, but increasingly the only, and so the natural answer. Anything that ran counter to these ideas was therefore by definition unnatural, and so wrong.

Given that markets were both about choice and enhancing the ability of individuals to choose, supplementing their rightness with ideas of democracy and rights was a simple step – again one that was suggested as being so simple it was natural. Bringing down barriers to trade became a moral as well a practical step: greater choices equalled greater personal freedom; greater personal freedom, and greater prosperity, in turn led to greater political choices. The movement from opening markets to establishing democracy looked transparent. Gordon Gekko, the leading character of Oliver Stone's *Wall Street*, famously remarked that greed is good. Less often remembered, but just as pertinent, was what he added: 'Greed is right, greed works.'[8]

Naturally, forces which promoted such freedoms were also right. So it was 'right' for Western companies to enter countries, regardless of whether their products were needed; 'right' for Western countries to demand that obstacles to trade be lowered or removed, not only because the people in those countries would become better off, but because they would eventually possess more freedoms and rights, ultimately – so the argument ran – including democratic ones.

With the notions of growth and markets thoroughly intertwined, it was soon being suggested that the metrics of one and the techniques of the other be applied to all manner of issues, from education (vouchers) to fisheries (individually transferable quotas), via privatization of state assets, expanding the use of public–private partnerships or introducing management performance targets into social services. Soon the ideas of economics – particularly that of 'utility maximization', or getting the greatest possible value from the least amount of expenditure – were being extended to other areas of life, from finding a partner to electing governments. Success begat success. As growth was achieved by business, the outcome was the 'businessization' of all manner of areas of society – the introduction of measurable targets into healthcare and education; the proliferation of PowerPoint presentations into every activity; endless talk of 'competitive advantage', 'branding', 'returns on investment' and 'exit strategies'.

After the crash

Then came the financial crisis of 2008. As governments bailed out banks and the extraordinary machinations of the sub-prime mortgage market came to light, it seemed for a brief period that the world stood on the brink of a new era – one in which finance and free market economics would never again be able to exert the influence they had in the previous two decades.

Two years on, we know that this was not the case. Despite the ensuing collapse in trade and deep recession across Europe and the United States, what is most striking about the global economy is just how little has changed in the way it is allowed to operate. For sure, there has been much discussion of the need for greater market oversight and regulation, but the idea that markets themselves should be the primary means by which societies realize their goals remains largely intact. And the reason for this is, of course, the continued primacy of what markets can deliver – economic growth.

Unless we can shake off our obsession with growth, we can be sure that the dominant element shaping the direction of policy making will remain the economic one, not just in matters relating directly to the economy but in all others as well – including environmental and ecological ones. Given this, it should not be surprising that the debates surrounding such crucial issues as climate change are not fronted by environmental scientists or climatologists, but by economists. And, following from this, that the main tools the world has so far invented for trying to reverse global warming are economic. (The irony of using a market instrument to cure the problems of what Nicholas Stern, himself an economist as well as the author of the *Stern Review on the Economics of Climate Change*, a report on climate change prepared for the UK government, labelled the world's greatest market failure – climate change – is seldom noted.)

In these debates we find at one extreme figures such as Bjørn Lomborg and his arguments that all we need is technology. At the other, are such mainstream thinkers as Paul Krugman, a Nobel laureate, who sees the problem as a straightforward one of using economic tools to guide us in the right direction, usually cutting greenhouse gas emissions via a cap-and-trade system or a carbon tax.[9]

In between are those who like to point out how the world's economies have tended to clean themselves up over time. At an early stage of development, most nations produce a lot of pollution. But once they reach a certain level of prosperity, people start putting a value on things like clean air and water; this turns into political pressure, which leads to regulation and eventually everyone is forced to clean themselves up.[10] It hardly seems worthwhile to notice that this kind of argument often masks special interests that would prefer not to pay clean-up costs immediately, especially if it will be someone else, such as the taxpayer, who eventually picks them up.

While there is some empirical evidence that such shifts may take place, to argue that such concepts make a case for doing less rather than more is to let the tail wag the dog. If pollution is brought down as countries grow richer, it is not just that a country can afford it, but because demand for pollution control grows stronger. Moreover, a far greater point is missed (one also ignored by Krugman and Lomborg), that we are not looking at a static or slowly changing situation involving just a single environmental variable, but a massive and absolute rise in resource use and environmental impact arising from billions of people reaching consumption thresholds. This is not a circumstance that can wait for countries to reach a certain level of development, it is an issue that has to be tackled before events take on a momentum of their own. Perhaps those living on continents far from the most polluted of Asia's industrial big cities fail to take into account the volume of damage already done.[11]

But regardless of the specific outlook of the participants in the debate, the environmental content continues to be viewed through an economic prism. Indeed, it is possible to draw a direct analogy between the way in which free markets go through their boom and bust cycle with the way environmental policy is pursued. Economies are super-charged by loading them with debt, then demanding they grow fast enough to repay their loans. If correctly calibrated, the loaned money should allow growth to proceed at a higher rate than would be achievable by just reinvesting profits. The temptation, however, is to take on more and more debt in a bid to make business turn over ever faster. Ultimately, the system becomes overloaded, the debt cannot be repaid, and there is a crash.

Exactly the same behaviour can be seen in the way free markets treat the natural environment. For more than two centuries, growth has been driven by taking more and more from nature. Throughout this period, the environmental depletion and deterioration that resulted was largely ignored; some problems were left untreated, others left for later and many, such as the increased amount of carbon dioxide in the atmosphere, simply not known about. Now, however, we have reached the point where the bills are coming due – but instead of paying them, we are pressing on, at an accelerating rate, demanding ever greater credit from nature.

As with the economy, crashes are part of this process, as a part of the environment becomes too stressed to continue. And much as it is those at the bottom of the economy who are usually the first to lose their jobs or their homes, so it is with the environment. When its systems fail, it is those on the margins of society who suffer most, finding their fields and water supplies poisoned or the forest they had patiently worked for years felled.

A different model

If we are to reject this economic view of the environment, we must question one of economics' core assumptions – that markets take account of things that people value by giving them a price.

This is not what happens. Markets only price in things that have prices in the first place. And from the start, industrial capitalism has taken advantage of things that had no price but which it could use – above all the environment and ecological services. Historically this can be attributed to capitalism's origins in Western Europe, in societies with abundant material resources but little skilled labour. Under such conditions, businesses were spurred on to develop technology that enhanced labour productivity, allowing fewer and fewer people to produce more and more things.

The one thing that was free in all this was the environment. Without having to pay to use air, and not having to pay much for water or other inputs, producers used these resources as if they did not matter. Even now, companies still largely act this way. Because of low prices for natural goods and ecological services, companies are encouraged to build their businesses by processing an ever greater volume of materials so they can sell an ever greater volume of whatever they make. This pushes them to develop technologies that allow one person to process more material – be it a miner extracting more coal, a factory worker assembling more computers or a farmer growing more crops – and then to push for ever greater consumption.

The American corn industry (or maize, as it is generally known in the US), exemplifies this approach. The US share of world corn production, at nearly 50 percent, stems from a relentless drive to achieve economies of scale. Mechanization allowed farmers to reduce the amount of labour they needed to raise crops; it also encouraged monocultures, which in turn encouraged the use of fertilizers and pesticides. As output soared, prices fell. Corn became so cheap it displaced other food staples. More and more uses were found for it in non-traditional areas – for example, as an animal feed, even for animals such as cows with no history of eating anything other than grass, and more recently as a biofuel ingredient.

With its output further supported by agricultural subsidies, the United States pressured other countries to open their markets to American corn. Even places with much lower labour costs found themselves unable to compete – perhaps because their landscapes were not suited to mechanization on the same scale as America, or they lacked the infrastructure necessary to support mechanization, or simply because they had a cultural preference for small farms worked intensively by more people.

In all this, however, the one thing that has not been priced in is corn's environmental impact. American farmers currently pay nothing for the carbon emissions they generate, either directly in transport or indirectly in the energy used to produce the fertilizers and pesticides they use. Pricing this in, along with making them pay more realistic prices for water and charging them for the impact of the chemicals they use, would significantly raise the cost of corn. This in turn would affect the meat industry (itself a free rider on the environment via livestock's emissions of greenhouse gases, its water intensity and often the carbon released by clearing forest – possibly more than transport in total).[12] The knock-on effect would then be felt in those industries indirectly benefiting from cheap grain, such as fast-food chains and makers of convenience foods.

Putting aside any discussion of whether people might be better off – or at least healthier – with fewer such food options, the emphasis on labour productivity encouraged by an underpricing of environmental resources has clearly played a huge role in determining the form of modern industry. In the American model, the incentives are aligned heavily in favour of a maximum throughput of resources. Once a production line is in place, then the goal is to move as much material through it as possible, using as few people as possible.

Such a model assumes that nature has an essentially limitless capacity, both to supply materials and absorb what people do to it. This is not to say that it gives its resources freely – land has to be farmed, minerals extracted, manufacturing organized, and so on – but it is to say that its bounty is abundant, and will remain that way. In the relatively sparsely populated world of the eighteenth and nineteenth centuries, that made sense for Americans. (Europeans, in contrast, had less need of such measures, being able to exploit the even cheaper resources available from their colonies.)

But it is a model that cannot be applied to the countries of Asia today. Many leading economists and pro-globalization advocates simply refuse to accept that the economic development model of the twentieth century is based on excluding environmental and social costs; that this model only more or less worked when only a relatively small proportion of the world population were using it; and by more or less we mean excluding the long-term damage to the world's environment that we are now having to confront.

This is not to say that continuing with current economic orthodoxy will end in catastrophe either rapidly or even for everyone. Despite the prophecies of doom made by many who have considered what climate change may have in store for the world, it is not the case that consumption-driven capitalism will inevitably lead to our world collapsing. It could, but what we are more likely to experience is something rather more insidious – a continual degradation and deterioration of the environment. For some, the costs will become apparent a lot earlier than for others. For others, there may be negligible costs, even in the medium term. Some courses of action may help to mitigate the impact, at least for some people. Efforts to reduce emissions of greenhouse gases, for example, look certain to be introduced in some form or another within the next several years.

Efforts merely to mitigate how humans behave within the current framework of consumption-driven capitalism, however, will almost certainly fail. Given human appetites, the incentives to keep on feeding those appetites, and the increasing number of people able to enjoy having their appetites fed, it is inconceivable that the absolute volume of what people consume will do anything but grow at a slower rate than it would with no attempts to make consumption more efficient.

So unless the cause of our environmental challenge is tackled, such efforts are likely to allow far more damage to take place than if we radically rethought such challenges now. That cause is what we consume – both its volume and its nature. The only way the world can expect to have an environment fit for those currently alive to live in, and to pass on to future generations in a decent form, is by consuming less and in a different way.

Asia confronts this issue first. If the countries of the region press forward with turbo-charged, consumption-fuelled growth, always looking to expand their economies at the maximum possible rate, then the environment will be overwhelmed. There is not the water, the land or the air to support such an economic programme.

If it were to be attempted, billions of people would be badly affected. Many would die – tens of millions? Hundreds of millions? It is impossible to say. As we are seeing with the floods that affected Pakistan in the summer of 2010, and the mudslides and other weather-driven events that are affecting China, people are already dying. It is not possible to draw a causal line between climate change and these deaths, but it is certainly a contributory factor. In the coming decades, it will become more so. And regardless of whether they die or not, billions of people across Asia can only be condemned to live in horrendously depleted environments.

Given this, those who refuse to acknowledge the contradiction between wanting to restrict human impact on the environment, particularly when it comes to global warming, while advocating the maintenance of a 'business as usual' approach that they say will end in prosperity for all are more than in denial. They are lying.

The Asian future

Paradoxically, the societies best placed to challenge and change the consumption-driven model are in Asia. The very size of the region's population, while apparently promising most for this model's continuation, in reality contains the seeds of its demise. This is because, no matter how technologically advanced or financially innovative humans become, our well-being and everything needed to sustain our societies depends on the productivity of natural systems. Asia, because of the scale of its populations, will run into the question of how to maintain the productivity of these systems in ways that nowhere else will. Indeed, because of the rapid rate of growth of China and India, it will occur far faster than almost anyone has yet recognized, driven by the adoption of consumption-driven capitalism. The biggest lie of all, therefore, is that consumption-driven capitalism can deliver wealth to all. In Asia it can only deliver short-term wealth to a minority; in the long term, it can only deliver misery to all. This is the intellectual dishonesty at the heart of the model the West has peddled to Asia.

Given the failure of Western countries to take responsibility for the future of the planet, it is now time for Asia to step up to the block. This is not to suggest that Asia has all the answers. But it is to say that Asia has a central responsibility for determining the world's fate. Either the countries of the region help to find solutions to the environmental problems confronting us, or they abdicate this role, quite possibly ensuring the world endures at best a deeply unpleasant future, and at worst the demise predicted in the grimmer forecasts of a far hotter planet made by scientists such as James Lovelock or James Hansen.[13]

In the wake of the global financial crisis, Asia's leaders have an opportunity and obligation to send out a different message – that measures to halt global warming and other pressing ecological concerns, far from being 'noble objectives' that can be postponed until the global economy is fixed, have to be the priority.

The good news is that there is time left to change. Despite the developments of recent decades, the majority of the population is still rural. Decisions that affect the future of these people's lives will perhaps be the most crucial of all – especially if alternative directions can be found that will prevent the migration to cities our current economic model demands.

In addition, leaders across the region are starting to question whether the Western model of consumption-driven capitalism is the answer to their countries' development needs. So far, most Asian leaders remain either unwilling or unsure how to articulate the dilemma they face, leading to a conspiracy of silence or, at best, a hope that solutions can be found later. Even in China, it will be a challenge to shape policies that reverse the globally interlocked economic development path of the last thirty years.

Of course, for Asians, it will be harsh to be told that as latecomers to the capitalist party they will never be able to attain the way of living taken for granted by most in the developed countries. But this is the message their leaders have to deliver: that no longer can the world live in denial; that new economic rules are needed; that limits to resource exploitation are necessary; that growth can no longer be our primary measure of success; and that governments will have to have the tools and strength to enforce constraints on those unwilling to accept them, be they companies or individuals.

Prosperity without growth?

This book is not anti-growth, nor does it advocate poverty. Certainly, prosperity without growth should be the planet's long-term goal, as eventually we must find ways of flourishing that do not require an ever-expanding use of resources. For now, however, that task should be left to the world's rich countries.

But this book's subject is not the rich world. It is about Asia, and the very different tasks Asian countries confront. Here, governments must produce growth while protecting ecological and social goods. The first of these tasks is accepting the reality of a growing population set to peak around mid-century. The poorest of these people must be lifted out of poverty to join all those others enjoying rich and fruitful lives.

But accepting that we must end poverty does not entail embracing fast-track growth. And so Asia's second task is refusing to heed all figures who call for consumption-driven economies, be they government leaders, officials at multilateral institutions such as the World Bank or IMF, policy makers, economists or any others. Their continued advocacy of the win-win proposition of globalization – that open markets and free trade allow fast-track development, which in turn leads to wealth 'trickling down' from the developed world to Asia, and then within the countries of Asia from richer people to poorer people – is simply wrong.

This will not happen. It cannot – because those who benefit from consumption-driven capitalism are not the consumers but businesses which have an incentive to focus on short-term gains regardless of their longer-term cost. The lie at the heart of consumption-driven capitalism is its claim that it delivers the best results – that more people become better off than in any other type of economic system. This claim is a lie because it masks the benefits that flow to corporate interests from continuing to evade the true environmental costs of their activities. Until now, countries have excluded environmental costs, accepting the damage that has ensued as being a necessary part of development. That cannot be allowed to continue. Only by including such costs can we create the incentives to change behaviour and so give our world a sustainable future.

Is this utopian? Absolutely not. Prosperity for all, both in Asia and elsewhere, is not a utopian goal, but one that is realizable with our abilities and know-how. In this, I am in total agreement with various of the arguments put forward by those such as Jeffrey Sachs – that for the expenditure of a relatively small amount of global income, the world can solve the problems of eradicating poverty, restricting population growth, and meeting the threat of irreversible and catastrophic climate change and other environmental catastrophes.

But we cannot do this unless we first prioritize pricing in the costs of the damage being done by the growth model that remains at the heart of all such proposals. Thus we absolutely *must* concentrate on ending poverty for the world's poorest. But to do this without paying adequate attention to the behaviour of the rich world and the two to three billion people in the developing world, especially Asia, who over the next two decades are set to move beyond subsistence and enter the consumption classes, will render all efforts at poverty alleviation meaningless. There is no point in raising people out of poverty to consume if their environment is not fit to live in.

We cannot think of development in terms of providing key infrastructure and a sound business environment, of promoting and disseminating modern science and technology, or even of offering social insurance, *unless* we have placed proper stewardship of the environment in first place.[14]

If we do not – if we continue to encourage consumption as being the motor which drives development – then we can only exacerbate the problem of providing proper environmental stewardship. We will have countries where people have mobile phones and falling water tables; with broadband internet and with rising levels of greenhouse gas emissions.

Only by putting environmental stewardship first, and living with the consequences of this decision, will we be able to create societies that can meaningfully tackle poverty alleviation in the long run. This book is about the steps we can take that will allow us to do both. The first step in this direction is for people in Asia to refuse to accept the dogma of Western economic theory, in particular the notion that markets are efficient and self-adjusting, can deliver prosperity to all, and can do so without imposing unbearable charges on large parts of our world. As latecomers to the model of development that puts a premium on wealth creation at any price, Asian countries will never be able to attain the ways of life taken for granted by most in the West. We must accept this to move beyond denial and look for alternatives – ones that by definition are better because they may have a chance of working.

Mobile phone subscriptions
Millions

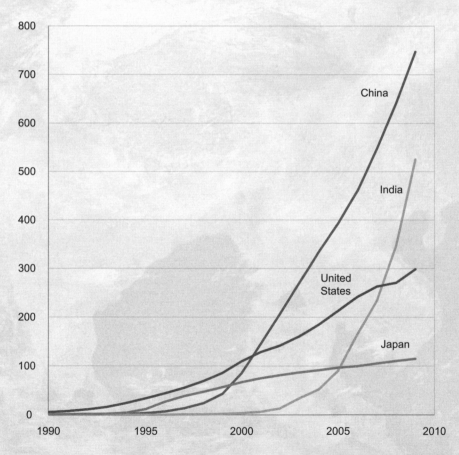

Source: International Telecommunications Union

1

ASIA ARRIVES – AND WANTS IT ALL

Asia stands at the threshold of consumption. Across China, India and south-east Asia, hundreds of millions of people are buying mobile phones and refrigerators, eating in McDonald's and KFC, and drinking Coke and Pepsi. But these are just the advance troops. Over the next decade and beyond, they will be joined by two to three billion more consumers, buying motorbikes and cars, upgrading to iPhones and high-definition TVs, and moving to cities where they can buy their own homes.

This is the dream that has kept Asia moving forward. Governments made fast-track growth a policy priority. They lowered barriers for multinational business. They told their populations that prosperity for all was achievable within a generation, maybe two at most. And the time to celebrate is almost here. The next few decades will see the most extraordinary jumps in the consumption of almost every product and service imaginable as Asia catches up.

Take poultry. This year, Americans will eat nine billion birds. As of today, the whole of Asia – thirteen times as many people as in the United States – eats sixteen billion birds annually. But if by 2050 each Asian was eating the same amount of poultry as each American does now, the region would eat its way through more than 120 billion birds.[1]

Or take energy. Today, the average American uses 250 kilowatt hours of power a day. In China, the average is 40 kilowatt hours, and in India it is 20 kilowatt hours. If Asia's population were to use as much energy per person as Americans, then they would consume fourteen times as much power as the United States does now. Even if Asia were to restrict itself to European energy levels – around 150 kilowatt hours per person per day – it would still use eight to nine times as much energy as America does now.

This prospect of a prosperous Asia excites many – those in business most of all. Be they car makers or coal miners, in insurance or IT, it would seem that Asia's huge market potential is finally materializing.

Governments are also pleased. At last, after two centuries of Western dominance, their region is regaining its position as the globe's economic centre of power. At the start of the nineteenth century, Asia accounted for over half the world's economic output. Over the next 150 years, its share plummeted as Europe and America rode the industrial revolution. In 1950, it accounted for just 18 percent. But now it is back. Driven first by Japan, then China and now also by India, by 2025 Asia should have half of world output, and by 2050 it will be back to its eighteenth-century heights of around 55 percent.

And then there are ordinary people. After decades of hard work and saving, hundreds of millions of people stand on the brink of middle-class abundance. Already enjoyed by Japan and the tiger economies of South Korea, Taiwan, Hong Kong and Singapore, now households across south-east Asia, China and India either have or have started acquiring the material trappings of affluence. For everyone, as Thomas Friedman puts it, the dream of living like Americans appears finally to be within reach.

Or is it? Those who think about the world's economic future – the World Bank, International Monetary Fund and other forecasters – see growth continuing uninterrupted. On current trends, they suggest world economic output is expected to grow between six and sevenfold between 2005 and 2050. (Jeffrey Sachs, for example, calculates that the world's gross product – the value of everything the world's economy produces – will rise by 6.5 times, or from $67 trillion to $420 trillion, between 2005 and 2050.[2]) Assuming that growth then slows in the second half of the century, it would end up between fifteen and twenty-five times bigger by the end of this century.[3]

A disproportionate share of the growth expected to come over that period would be in Asia. Currently, the countries of the region account for some $30 trillion of world product; by 2050, averaging real growth of just over 5 percent a year, that would be at least $230 trillion – between seven and eight times greater than now.

These are astonishing numbers. But they demand scrutiny. According to Lester Brown, the president of the Washington-based Earth Policy Institute, an environmental research body, up until the middle of the twentieth century the world more or less lived within its means. Then it embarked on a three-decade growth spurt, expanding its economy eightfold. Around 1980, it passed the earth's regenerative capacity – and now it stands at somewhere approaching 30 percent beyond our planet's sustainable capacity.[4]

This does not mean that the world stands on the brink of collapse. It has enormous reserves that humanity can tap into for decades to come at current rates of extraction. But if we push the world's economy towards being six or seven times bigger than now, or fifteen times, or twenty-five times, we can be sure that more and more of those resources will be driven to the point of collapse. The region where these collapses will have the most immediate and greatest impact will be Asia.

Water is its most pressing resource issue. Almost without exception, countries across Asia are seeing the amount of water available to each of their citizens fall sharply. India's per capita renewable water resources fell 7 percent from 2000 to 2005, China's by 5 percent.[5] Both country's problems pale into insignificance compared with Pakistan's. Agriculture is the economy's biggest sector, employing nearly half the working population and accounting for a quarter of GDP – and 96 percent of all water withdrawals. This extraction is destroying the country's water resources. According to the United Nations World Water Assessment Programme, per capita renewable water resources fell by more than half in the first five years of this century – from 2961 cubic metres in 2000 to 1420 cubic metres in 2005.[6]

Across the region, countries find themselves with less water – and with more of what they do use being pumped out of aquifers faster than rain replenishes them. How can it make sense, then, to pursue ways of life such as replacing the vegetarianism traditional to much of India with eating beef and other meats that require much greater quantities of water to produce a meal? Current extraction rates have created a 'water bubble' economy, where consumption now will deny resources to the next generation.

Other resources are equally threatened. Without a change of heart within the next decade, forests in Asia will be lost to the point where most people will never have the chance to see what covered most of the region's tropical landscape just sixty years ago. Brazil's deforestation of the Amazon is well known. But Indonesia's clearing of its forests is far more advanced. In the last fifty years its rainforest cover has fallen from 82 percent of the country to less than half.[7] Its impact on the world has been almost as great as that of Brazil. Between 1990 and 2005, the latter's forest clearance contributed almost one third of all carbon dioxide emissions attributable to deforestation. Indonesia was not far behind – responsible for more than one quarter of all such emissions. Asia as a whole was responsible for nearly 36 percent of such emissions – a greater source than Brazil.[8]

And climate change eventually will outstrip even water shortages in terms of its impact on the environment. It is hard to know which country will be most affected, but Bangladesh, and its population of 160 million, will be a candidate. In its 2007 report, the UN's Intergovernmental Panel on Climate Change estimated that by 2050 Bangladesh's agricultural output could be sharply less than it is now, with rice output dropping 8 percent and wheat by 32 percent.[9] Already the World Bank forecasts that developing countries will need to spend a total of $40 to $100 billion every year from now until 2050 on adapting to the effects of climate change on their farming sectors.

Similar statistics as those for water, forests and food can be found for almost every other critical resource – from topsoil to rare earths, from greenhouse gas emissions to crude oil. Already, either sources are falling to dangerously low levels or exploiting them is having an environmental impact that threatens the livelihoods of huge numbers of people.

Adhering to current policies of consumption-fuelled growth may bring middle-class affluence to many people across Asia – hundreds of millions, probably, perhaps more. But their ranks will be far outnumbered by the many more across the region, especially those living in rural areas or recent migrants to Asia's ever-growing number of mega-cities, whose lives will be devastated by a lack of water and desertification, extreme weather, rising sea levels and the other impacts of climate change and environmental degradation. For them, the era of American consumption will never arrive.

At the limits

Of course, there are those who dismiss such forecasts as Malthusian fear-mongering. After all, predictions that the world would run into limits have turned out to be repeatedly false over the last two centuries. Instead, time after time, human ingenuity has come up with new ways of extracting more value – most obviously in agriculture, where the 'green revolution' of the 1960s and 1970s has provided food for billions of people in the developing world.

And what about perhaps the most famous forecast ever that the world was running out of resources – *The Limits to Growth* report issued by the Club of Rome in the early 1970s? It, too, predicted that continuing growth in consumption levels combined with rising populations would inevitably lead to a resource-depleted world of shortages. But such constant predictions of ever more intense resource shortages leading to rising commodity prices have likewise been proven wrong – prices have consistently fallen. Our energy sources, especially oil, remain as abundant as ever, despite an unceasing series of 'peak' forecasts.

But, while acknowledging that countless previous forecasts have turned out to be wrong, my point is different. Over the last 200 years, since Thomas Malthus was writing, limits have been surpassed time and time again, enabling the economic growth of the twentieth century. But to focus on shortages and depletion alone is to miss the bigger issue – the impact the use of those resources has had on our environment, and above all the fact that such environmental costs have been excluded from goods that use those resources. Thus industry was encouraged to develop products and use techniques for which it did not have to pay a true price.

So, while I also believe that humanity will continue to come up with ideas and inventions that will allow us to produce enough food to feed everyone, the way in which we do this – and produce all the other goods and services we consume – will have to change. The ecological cost of human activity must now be taken into account. Where limits are being approached that threaten catastrophe for communities or populations constraints must be imposed, be it through outright bans or giving them a price via taxes or other charges. Malthus was not wrong when he said that if things continued as they were, limits would be reached. And the *Limits to Growth* report was not wrong in saying that on then-current consumption trends the world would run up against a range of limits. It is worth noting that the trends forecast by *Limits to Growth* have remained largely unchanged, and a recent analysis of its predictions found them broadly in line with events over the nearly forty years since the report was published.[10]

What is really strange, therefore, is the assumption that limits can always be overcome, and that the impact of using those resources can also be ignored. As with much else that has passed for conventional thought in today's world, a good part of the responsibility for this can be laid at the door of market fundamentalism – in particular, its claim that at the heart of what markets do lies the notion of 'efficiency' by arranging for the best possible distribution of a finite amount of goods via a free market. In the short term, many possible arrangements can be made that make people better off – inventing machines that can pump water from ever deeper within aquifers, for example. However, if these ignore longer-term depletion issues, such as where the water will be found to raise crops for the next generation, Malthusian concerns have only been deferred, not solved.

Off a cliff

But if putting a tricky problem off until later is at least understandable, what can be made of embracing a problem that can only get worse?

In 1990, China had a negligible car industry, producing just a few hundred thousand vehicles. In 2009, it surpassed the United States to become the world's biggest auto market, with some thirteen million vehicles sold. Growth is expected to continue, driven by an enormous expansion of factories built by almost every one of the world's automotive companies. A study prepared for the US Department of Energy estimates that China's total vehicle stock will catch up with that of the United States in the late 2020s, when both countries will have around 330 million vehicles. It will then rise to between 470 million and 660 million by mid-century – not far off the 820 million or so vehicles in the world's total vehicle fleet today.

What fuel will power all these vehicles? In 2005, China's vehicle fleet used 109 million tonnes of oil; by 2050, it will need between six and ten times as much. Finding sources for this will be hard: 'Considering the rapid depletion of the world's oil reserve … and the geopolitical complications of global oil supply and demand, the study results suggest that unmanaged vehicle growth and only incremental improvements in vehicle efficiency will lead to an unsustainable and unstable transportation system in China.'[11]

Other studies come to the same conclusion. Another American report, produced for the Council for Foreign Relations, projected that if China's per capita oil consumption were to reach that of South Korea's now, the country's share of world oil consumption would rise from its current 10 percent to 70 percent. Alternatively, if China's share of world oil consumption were to peak at 22 percent – America's current level – world oil output would have to rise by 13 percent a year for the next decade, or thirteen times the 1 percent growth rate averaged since 1975.[12]

Clearly the companies investing in China's automobile industry hope something will turn up along the way that will change things. A taste of what that could be comes from Carlos Ghosn who, as head of both

France's Renault and Japan's Nissan, is among those investors.

Ghosn envisages massive growth for the automotive industry. Helped by China, India and other developing economies, he forecasts that by 2050 the world will have 2.9 billion passenger cars, more than four times its current figure.[13] He acknowledges that those cars will be different from those of today – they will be zero-emission vehicles. But apart from this nod to sustainability, he has nothing to say about the other resource and environmental issues such an industry would create: the materials to make them, the infrastructure for them to be driven on, the fuel to run them, or the congestion and other external costs they would impose on the societies that had to endure them.

Across Asia, similar short-term visions abound. The demands on resources, the stresses caused by pollution and the impact on climate are accelerating, and are likely to accelerate further. Technology may have helped the world feed itself, but it has created the means for companies to act without proper analysis of the consequences. Fishing and forestry technology allowing harvesting on hitherto unimaginable scales are two examples of this. But perhaps even more dangerous is the technology that has transformed the speed with which capital flows around the globe. High-speed financial transactions have encouraged the growth of consumption by offering new ways of spending to individuals, such as credit and debit cards and other forms of consumer debt, and providing an ever wider range of financial services to corporations. These have accelerated the speed at which decisions and actions can be taken to exploit resources.

Sustainable development

To meet the array of environmental and ecological challenges it faces, what Asia must find are ways of making its economies sustainable – ones that 'meet the needs of the present without compromising the ability of future generations to meet their own needs', to quote the UN's defining statement in the Brundtland Commission report, published in 1987.[14]

An important point about sustainability is that it does not require things to remain unchanged. We have to preserve vital ecosystems. Resources can be depleted provided we ensure there are other things that can perform a similar function for future generations, either directly (there is something else that can be used in its place) or indirectly (via an idea or invention that makes a previous resource redundant).

The key point is that rather than stimulating growth, countries should be looking at the sustainability of their productive bases. What impact will growth have? How is it possible to encourage forms of growth that maintain productive sustainability while barring those that undermine it?

Understanding the relationship between these questions is helped enormously by a simple but elegant equation, I=PAT, first formulated in the early 1970s by biologist Paul Ehrlich and environmentalist John Holdren. I=PAT highlights how the impact of humans on the environment (I) is determined by multiplying population size (P), by affluence (A) and the level of environmental impact per unit of spending (T), otherwise known as the level of technological development.

In Asia the size of P is enormous, but populations change only slowly over time, allowing us to bracket it for now and instead concentrate on the other elements affecting environmental impact – A, which we want to see rise, and T, which we want to fall. Basic maths suggests that if we want people's affluence to double, and the environmental impact to remain unchanged, then T would have to halve.

Currently, Asian consumption levels are around a twentieth of America's. To raise them to, say, half of American levels, would mean raising A tenfold. To keep the environmental impact at current levels, therefore, would require lowering the environmental impact per unit of spending by 90 percent.

Frankly, this is inconceivable. As industry expands, and cars, home appliances and other electrical goods become ever more commonplace, the environmental impact of rising affluence will only increase – regardless of the growing efficiency with which goods are made and electricity generated. A's rise will far offset T's fall.

So if countries across Asia want to keep the impact on their environment within manageable limits, as well as addressing T they will also have to look at A, and ask whether there are other ways of being affluent than those assumed until now. In Chapter 3, I explore possible ways of finding alternative sources of affluence. For now, however, I want to explore one further implication of the difference in relationship between A and T in the developed world and in Asia.

For the rich countries, the pressing environmental issue remains climate change, and what can be done to reduce greenhouse gas emissions without having to make any sacrifices in ways of life. As most of these countries have populations that are stable or falling, the challenge therefore is maintaining or slightly improving their current level of affluence while hoping that technology will allow them to lower T, so lessening their overall impact on the environment.

Grasping this explains why Western countries still see little need to change their behaviour – for them, climate change is still a technological issue. But it also explains why Western countries have so great a difficulty in understanding what has to be done in Asia – quite simply, they still fail to grasp that Asia cannot use the same tools as them, nor that Asia will have to go down a very different path from the one they have taken.

Failing to see this last point may partially explain why Western proposals on ways to help developing countries in Asia and elsewhere so often miss the point. If Asia were to find an alternative development route, the interests of many Western businesses would be severely affected. Western economic policy towards Asia may not be as explicitly aimed at exploiting the region as it was during the colonial era, but it remains focused on maintaining Western economic advantage, nowhere more so than in support of multinational companies.

From the 1980s onwards, market fundamentalism's international arm, globalization, prised markets open, allowing companies to sell more goods and transfer manufacturing operations to locations with lower-paid and usually non-unionized workers. Weaker regulatory systems also allowed for the offshoring of polluting and other environmentally costly facilities.[15]

Companies often found the pickings richest in countries that had just liberalized their economic systems – in such places, markets preceded regulation, creating the conditions for a bonanza in the exploitation of natural goods such as forests or wildlife. Forests in south-east Asia, for example, have been felled more quickly in newly democratic countries than in authoritarian ones, precisely because once private companies were able to secure a foothold they had both the motive and usually the means, such as access to capital and equipment, to act as fast as they could.[16]

The financial crisis has done nothing to weaken the beneficiaries of globalization. Indeed, it probably had the opposite effect: with their home economies in recession, multinationals had even greater reasons for expanding their operations in countries where they expected growth, notably Asia. Foreign investment into India expanded each year through the crisis, while China's held broadly steady at around $90 billion a year.

Of course, this still leaves Western countries facing the dilemma that supporting their model of economic development in Asia simultaneously worsens the prospect of finding a solution to climate change. But then again, that might also be because the world is becoming increasingly aware that the planet's climate future will be determined at least as much by Asia as by the rich countries. Indeed, what is decided in the capitals of North America and Europe will be irrelevant if China and India are not brought on board. And if Asia does opt to allow consumption-driven development to take precedence, they will have little say in the key decisions determining how high temperatures, and with them sea levels, will go.

There is a certain irony in this. As little as fifteen years ago, few people in the West (or Asia) envisaged a world in which countries such as China and India might actually be rich. For sure, business executives would talk about the potential of such markets, but there was little expectation that it would be realized in anything but the long term. The speed with which these countries have grown their economies has caught many people off balance.

Indeed, now they can see what impact this growth is having, many in the West are already ruing the rapid economic growth of these two countries. Some of the reactions to China's re-emergence betray the underlying resentment of this new reality – because of the shift in economic power it represents, and because of the fears it brings about being forced to share the world's resources. Assuming India follows in China's footsteps, such resentment is likely to grow even more severe.

Fear of speaking out

So just why is it that no one wants to stand up and say to Asians that they cannot have it all? One reason was alluded to at the start of this chapter – the idea of having it all is very appealing. Pandering to people's aspirations, however, is the easy way to go. The biggest reason for avoiding the truth is fear – fear of the terrible consequences of standing up and telling everyone that, quite simply, they cannot have it all.

Even those with no vested interests appear to find it difficult to state the obvious. Among the various outpourings on the global financial crisis, one of the clearest-eyed commentators is Joseph Stiglitz. In *Freefall*, his analysis of what went wrong in America from the Reagan era onwards, he explicitly condemns his country's way of life, and warns off others trying to emulate it: 'The US lifestyle is not sustainable … If those in the developing countries try to imitate America's lifestyle, the planet is doomed. There are not enough natural resources, and the impact on global warming would be intolerable.'[17]

He makes a strong case for markets being the wrong tools for achieving social objectives. Yes, they can help allocate resources efficiently, but the total failure of 'efficient market theory', as put into practice in the years before the financial crisis, starkly revealed how much America had used its power and influence at home and abroad to create an economic system that supported the self-interest of a small number of its institutions.

And yet his arguments peter out. No substantive new thinking emerges on what the United States should do about this, let alone where this leaves the rest of the world. The problem is that better regulations, even ones that worked, would not confront the issues of America's unsustainable lifestyle. But much as Jeffrey Sachs avoids talking about the need to transform lifestyles among the already well off in both the rich and the developing world, preferring to focus on the needs of the poor, so Stiglitz cannot move beyond an economics that remains essentially rooted in free markets, just with better regulation. In the final pages of his book, he nods to the possibility of there being other, greater goals that require attention: 'The failures in our financial system are emblematic of broader failures in our economic system, and the failures of our economic system reflect deeper problems in our society.'

He then suggests that the rules of the game have changed globally, and that 'Washington consensus policies and the underlying ideology of market fundamentalism are dead'. If only this were true. The unnerving thing about the financial crisis is not what happened, or even what it revealed, but just how much of what caused it remains intact. Why then, does Stiglitz claim the opposite?

I suspect it has a connection with the fact that standing up and saying something as radical as that the people of Asia cannot have it all would open the way to saying that the people of the rich world cannot have it all either.

Free market thinking allows those in the rich world to pretend that their lifestyles are OK because everyone else can aspire to them too. But if people in the developing world cannot have such lifestyles – because the demands they place on global resources are too great – then those in the rich world turn out to be no better than their colonial predecessors who believed in European superiority.

It is for these reasons of supposed neutrality that the West, even at its more liberal end, continues to promote the idea that liberal democracy and liberal markets, whatever their shortcomings in practice, contain universal truths. For if these ideas hold true everywhere and so are applicable to all, then there is no reason to question the basis of their wealth, nor the right of their companies to go out and obtain more of it around the world. This is the ideology which is still being fed into Asia, via calls from newspaper commentators for open markets, via economists promising ever greater prosperity, and via officials calling for ever-increased consumption.

It is understandable, therefore, that governments across Asia still fail to recognize – or refuse to accept – that the same free market thinking that pushed the economies of the United States and Europe into financial crisis is creating the conditions for a series of ecological and political crises whose long-term impact will far outstrip the market collapse of 2008.

The costs will not be so instantly apparent as a sharp fall in stock market prices. But they are already being paid. With growing levels of affluence, hundreds of millions of Asians are enjoying a new life of abundance, but one steeped in over-consumption and wastage. In India, still home to a significant number of undernourished people, well over half the women between 20 and 69 years old are overweight. In China, approaching 90 million people are already clinically obese, with forecasts suggesting the number will rise to 200 million by 2015, and that within two decades two out of three people in the country will be overweight or obese, the same proportion as in the United States now.[18]

Governments continue to allow traditional practices, often frugal ones, to be pushed aside. In India, more and more people are replacing vegetarian diets with meat ones, much to the satisfaction of the food industry. Average meat consumption per person is currently six grammes a day; the Ministry of Food Processing Industries sees that rising to fifty grammes within a decade or so. 'When such phenomenal increase in meat consumption occurs,' says a ministry spokesperson, 'the sector will witness a tremendous growth.'[19]

Governments are, however, finding it harder to ignore the almost inevitable conflicts that will arise over resources. Already, water flowing from the Himalayas is a major cause of tension. At one end, India and Pakistan are clashing over rivers flowing through Kashmir. At the other, Vietnam is becoming increasingly worried about Chinese, Lao and Thai plans to build dams along the upper Mekong that could severely affect water flow in the river's lower reaches. In the East China Sea, Japan and China are arguing over oil and gas fields. Six countries contest ownership of parts of the South China Sea, with energy and fishing resources a major interest. East Asian nations fret about securing sea lanes across the Indian Ocean and through south-east Asia, vital links for the oil and gas they buy from Africa and the Middle East. Across the region, such disputes over resources, both real and potential, can only worsen if countries continue to make fast-track economic growth their principal goal.

Non-consumer choices

Wherever we look, therefore, wanting it all can only result in trouble. It is not that Asia stands at a turning point; too many difficult decisions lie ahead for any one to be singled out as vital. But the countries of the region must start paying more attention to the environmental and resource implications of their policy choices.

For two centuries Asia did little choosing; the Western colonial powers dominated the region, exploiting its people and resources for their own benefit. After the Second World War, many countries found themselves choosing between capitalism and communism, though for many people the choice was forced upon them rather than freely taken. In the 1980s and 1990s, it seemed that finally countries could choose whether to embrace free markets. Except that this also was not really a choice; it was accepting orthodoxy.

But despite the shortcomings of that orthodoxy having now been demonstrated, no one is proposing alternatives. After a brief pause for rhetoric, the countries of the West have resumed their old ways, struggling to cope with the economic fallout of the financial crisis. Europe has adopted austerity, with the implicit promise that as long as populations can endure several years of belt-tightening their way of life should be maintainable. The United States, despite Barack Obama's promises of change, continues to search for ways of having it all.

Under such circumstances, Asia can expect to hear more urgings to be responsible, reduce its emissions, enforce pollution laws and continue trying to grow its economies. The incoherent policy responses arising from this urging of growth on the one hand and restraint on the other will then be condemned as inadequate – either for governments failing to take the global challenge of climate seriously, or for not liberalizing their economies fast enough.

Decisions, conflicts

Throughout history, humans have recognized that their individual rights are not absolute. In particular, people have accepted that at times of duress, they may have to surrender their freedoms and work for a common good. Even under normal circumstances, sacrifices and restraint may also be called for, as establishing and maintaining a stable society requires people to consider the impact their actions could have on others.

Such notions have been replaced. Particularly in the West, entitlement rights and the pursuit of self-interest are the prevailing beliefs. No longer do people need to adapt themselves to the needs of society or others. Instead, things must be changed to suit them. Consequently, even under a threat so severe as climate change, there is no need for people to change their way of life. In a world where people's wants are met by a market in which others benefit from meeting those wants, there are no limits, and so, no need for sacrifices.

We must acknowledge that there are decisions which have to be taken – that there are not, despite the fervent wishes of so many people, only win-win outcomes. It is the blindness – wilful blindness, I would suggest – of those who only advocate win-win outcomes that I want to highlight.

There are major conflicts that have to be resolved – between what we can expect immediately, and what we want in the longer term; that what countries in Asia have to do is different from what the countries of the West have to do; that what Asia does may impinge on some extremely powerful vested interests, most of which are Western in origin and have strong backers in Western-influenced bodies.

As we discover what limits the world imposes on us, we must also ask what limits we must place on ourselves – and choose which limits we want. Nowhere has to choose more urgently than Asia. If the countries of the region are to create a future for themselves within ecological limits, then they must figure out what they should not be doing.

The prerequisite for this is to stop looking to the West for inspiration. The rich countries are not ignoring the challenge, but their preoccupations are very different from those of developing Asia. The issue confronting the rich countries is whether they can reduce their ecological impact while broadly maintaining their current ways of living. The measures they eventually take may need to be drastic, but whether this will be the case remains unknown. Consequently their debates principally focus for now on mitigating their impact on the environment rather than radically changing the way people live.

What these debates fail to address is what is happening in the rest of the world. They acknowledge that solutions to climate change will have to include the big developing countries – Russia and Brazil, as well China and India. And, particularly since the collapse of the Copenhagen climate talks, there is an awareness that these countries' interests make coming up with a global answer an extremely difficult task. Perhaps because of this, when the issues facing the rest of the world are considered – which aside from demonizing China, is not often – the suggestions made are cosmetic.

Asia must question the solutions that emanate from such bodies and interests, especially those that suggest that the world's long-term future can be trusted to technologies and investments which posit the continuation of consumption-driven economies. This is still thinking in terms of the same kinds of outcome – a world in which the richer nations are a little constrained, but the poorer ones are brought up in the same model.

Unfortunately, the way in which governments across the region think about such questions, when they consider them at all, remains rooted in conventional ways of thinking – the one that says that people across Asia can aspire to the same consumption-fuelled lifestyles now experienced by Americans, and that if they do, then their governments will benefit from the power and prestige of a re-emerged Asia.

And yet neither of these are credible goals. Attempting to realize them can only end in environmental catastrophe. Those who suggest that technological and financial ingenuity will be able not just to avert disaster but allow people to move towards a consumption-fuelled lifestyle are living in a dream world, as the next chapter explains.

Carbon dioxide emissions per capita
Tonnes

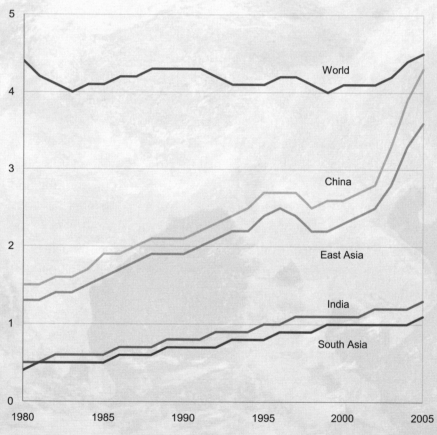

Source: World Resources Institute

2

CLUTCHING AT STRAWS

Conventional economic wisdom has it that humans are rational: *Homo economicus* always acts to improve his or her well-being. The edifice of economic thought is built on the narrow foundation of this assumption. But with much of the architecture underpinning the West's financial system now shown to be of appalling design, relying on such a narrow base looks deeply irrational.

Should we therefore be paying more attention to the still-emerging school of behavioural economics that seeks to explain – rationally, of course – how irrational behaviour can also affect economic decision-making? Possibly, because then we might start understanding why it is that when it comes to tackling global environmental perils, Western experts and their Asian disciples continue to rely on the tools of *Homo economicus*.

In almost every discussion on what to do about climate change, markets, finance and technological innovation are the three must-haves, wheeled out time and time again by governments and heavyweight commentators in the opinion pages of the *New York Times, Financial Times, The Economist* and *Wall Street Journal*.

Market fundamentalism tightened its grip on public and learned opinion through the 1990s and 2000s. In turn, similar capitalism-inspired ideas have also become an integral part of environmental thought. Veterans of the green movement such as Amory Lovins in the US and the UK's Jonathon Porritt began talking about what markets have to offer in the struggle to reverse the world's resource and environmental crises.[1]

It seems as if everyone – bar a handful of extremist environmentalists and academics – feels that progress can only be realized by accepting the dominance of capitalism.

Certainly, there are differences on exactly what mix of innovation, market incentives and financial tools offers the best way forward, but few people seem willing to question the assumption that we should continue to look at markets as a source for answers to capitalism's failings.

Wherever we look around the world, conventional economic thinking remains the principal source of solutions. Somehow, it is suggested, we must find ways of harnessing those forces that have got us into such trouble – self-interest and greed, harnessed to technology – to get us out.

This reliance on conventional economic thinking amounts to clutching at straws. *Homo economicus* is a rational figure in theory, but has turned out to be the source of madness in reality, constantly urging us on to further heights of consumption and resource abuse. Calls to invest more in technology, to find new financial tools that allow us to speculate on carbon, or simply to rely on corporate self-interest, can only distract us from the search for real answers. And in the context of environmental problems triggered by economic growth models, Asia would be most irrational to have faith that markets, technology and financial innovation will come up with viable solutions.

To understand why this is, we need to look at the underpinnings of each of these three factors and reveal how claims of their value as purveyors of future solutions mask vested interests – vested interests that will resist any differing opinions.

Market failings

The great thing about markets, suggests Paul Krugman, is that they 'create decentralized incentives to do the right thing'.[2] We know what the right thing is: creating sustainable societies by slashing the environmental impact of humanity. So how exactly do the markets do this or create incentives to do this?

Advocates of markets say the answer can be found in their unique ability to supply products and services that meet people's wants and needs at the best possible price. Supported by a minimal legal infrastructure to guarantee property rights and contracts, markets provide the incentive for companies and individuals to harness the resources of people, materials and capital to produce whatever the world wants in the most efficient and effective manner. Societies that embrace markets can be guaranteed ever-increasing productivity.

Of course, markets have their shortcomings. Sometimes monopolies emerge, or commons such as fisheries, forests and the biosphere are over-exploited. These, however, are the exceptions, advocates claim. Overall, the benefits of innovation and the delivery of ever more goods and services far outweigh the occasional headache markets throw up. This belief lies at the heart of the idea that markets will eventually find a solution to environmental and resource problems.

Perhaps the biggest fan of the markets' ability to solve environmental problems is Thomas Friedman, the *New York Times* columnist, who having preached the benefits of globalization in *The World is Flat,* now puts his faith in the same force of self-interest to save the world from climate change:

The only engine big enough to impact Mother Nature is Father Greed: the Market. Only a market, shaped by regulations and incentives to stimulate massive innovation in clean, emission-free power sources can make a dent in global warming.[3]

And who better to power that greed than the mother of all consumers, the United States:

An Earth Race led by America – built on markets, economic competition, national self-interest and strategic advantage – is a much more self-sustaining way to reduce carbon emissions than a festival of voluntary, nonbinding commitments at a UN conference. Let the Earth Race begin.[4]

The leap of faith this calls for is prodigious, almost religious. For markets to deliver the solutions Friedman believes they can requires we forget most of what happened between 2007 and 2009, the last time we were told to rely on capitalism's inherent ability to self-correct. Once again we must accept that greed is good. We are asked to believe that market forces, harnessing competition and self-interest, while subjected to the lightest touch of government regulation, will convert the world's most profligate nation into its saviour.

This is a step too far. 'The [global financial] crisis,' writes Joseph Stiglitz, 'should lay to rest any belief in "rational" markets. The irrationalities evident in mortgage markets, in securitization, in derivatives and in banking are mind-boggling; our supposed financial wizards have exhibited behaviour which, to use the vernacular, seemed "stupid" even at the time.'[5]

Would we want to trust the future of our planet to a phenomenon that encourages people to be stupid? Of course not.

The notion that markets deliver 'the right thing' stems from Adam Smith's insight that competition between self-interested producers will lead to the maximum amount of goods being made available at the lowest possible prices, thus benefiting both manufacturers and consumers. It follows, naturally, that if these benefits are shared by a majority of the population and keep growing, then societies that use markets are likely to have widespread popular support.

However, the fact that self-interest on both the demand and supply side of market-based societies has produced such powerful results around the world does not mean that these results are always optimal to those societies – especially over time. Societies have benefited from markets, particularly when it comes to the breadth and depth of goods and services available, but the ultimate impact of this system has not been felt yet, particularly not on an environmental level.

Perhaps most importantly, markets are silent on the distribution of wealth and the privileges this brings. As some institutions or individuals acquire greater wealth, they can set about protecting and enhancing their positions, leading to the emergence of powerful vested interests. In extreme instances, monopolies result. More common is the straightforward lobbying for support in the form of subsidies or continued protection from having to pay for the costs of pollution or environmental degradation.

All automotive companies, for example, are supported by massive government funding on roads and transport infrastructure. The world's airlines are exempt from paying taxes on aviation fuel. And almost no coal-mining company has ever paid the full cost of cleaning up after its operations, let alone the health bills of those affected by particulates and other toxic materials released from burning coal.

Markets do not self-correct for any of these failures. If societies want to correct such problems they have to look to external forces, such as taxation or laws backed by enforcement; greed is not the solution. Rather, it is the problem.

Corporations, not society

Another rarely mentioned aspect of markets is that their principal beneficiaries are not consumers but companies and their owners. Of course, companies are not all bad news. Since the onset of industrial capitalism, they have been the drivers of growth. Their organization of production brings benefits to a huge range of people: their staff and suppliers; those who benefit from the tax revenues they generate; and the customers who like or need their products. All these have an interest in the continued existence of companies and can be regarded as 'stakeholders' in the contemporary way of doing business.

Nonetheless, all these benefits, regardless of their enormous total size, are ancillary. Companies in themselves have a very narrow range of interests, extending no further than ensuring their continued existence and growth. Unlike human beings, they have no interest in whether the environment is degraded or whether the resources they use will not be available for future generations. Their goal is to produce strong short-term results. To do this they need growth, both of themselves and of the economies in which they operate.

Unable to stand still, they strive for increases both in absolute volume of output and relative productivity, making more and doing so more efficiently.[6] Periodically, the economic system in which they operate crashes but, as we saw in 2008–09, the inevitable response is for governments to initiate programmes aimed at stimulating consumption in order to get companies back to producing more. Countries that have stumbled on growth formulas have done phenomenally well, recycling their wealth via innovation in further sources of growth. But they have also locked themselves on a treadmill.

Under the rules of capitalism developed in the nineteenth century by Europe, then refined in the twentieth century by America, this treadmill has both grown and turned ever faster. It has been driven by the discovery of ever more sources of power, and has acquired the most extraordinary ability to generate material objects. But to do so, companies have required the most fantastic volume of resources. At the end of the twentieth century, making a car produced as much pollution as would driving that car for a decade, along with waste weighing nearly thirty times as much as its weight.[7]

By their very nature, companies devour resources in order to meet their production needs. So to expect them to come up with any meaningful solutions for resolving the resource depletion and environmental degradation they create is to mistake what they do.

That Asia might threaten such a model is the kind of thought that companies prefer to ignore. That its sheer size and already overstressed environment may make it impossible to continue using resources in ways that the twentieth-century world could only just cope with is an issue that most executives find it easier simply not to address. Instead, the sheer size of its population, and the potential this offers for growth, silences all doubts.

Of course, few companies expect their futures in the region to be easy. Where sizeable markets are emerging, as in China, the competition is phenomenal, both between multinationals and with domestic companies. This competition has a dramatic effect on the environment as businesses look for short cuts to secure immediate competitive advantages. Already many companies must suspect that their quest for long-term profits may prove futile. Still, however, they think of these countries only in terms of market logic; that other limits may have a role continues to be ignored. The only course of action is to press on; factories must be built, technology and know-how transferred and market share pursued. Under corporate logic, there really is no alternative.

No self-greening

Arguments that companies should 'go green' because doing so would be good for them are always unwarranted. Companies prefer to claim they are going green, appropriating terms such as 'sustainable' and 'green' in an effort to sound responsible.

The most egregious example may be the claim of mining companies to be producing 'clean coal'. Coal can never be clean. Its mining and burning can only result in pollution and carbon dioxide emissions. These can be partially controlled, but only at great cost. Most countries that rely on coal to provide them with energy will have to continue using this fuel to some extent, and so will have to work with mining companies. But the companies themselves, rather than spending money on finding cleaner ways to mine and burn coal, instead prefer to take the far cheaper path of lobbying for lower restrictions and higher subsidies, and putting out publicity claiming their activities are not really all that harmful. Their interests continue to be inherently very different from those of the societies in which they operate – a fact which they do their best to obscure.[8]

In the few cases where corporate 'greening' is meaningful, it is almost always because of other benefits that accrue to a company, such as cost savings or public relations.

Take Coca-Cola. It has announced ambitious recycling plans with the goal of recovering around half of all its bottles and cans by 2015. To help it reach this target, in 2009 it announced the launch of the world's largest PET recycling plant in South Carolina, US. Costing $50 million, the plant will eventually have the capacity to recycle enough plastic for two billion twenty-ounce bottles a year.

Impressive? No. The majority of the plastics used in this plant will be bought from other sources, rather than the containers that the company recovers. Moreover, even if the plant used plastics derived exclusively from its own containers, output would be a small fraction of what it wants to sell in China – where its target for 2020 is tripling its current sales to 120 billion units. Clearly its ambition to grow its sales volume far outstrips its ambition to deal with the impact of its product packaging, rendering its recycling goal essentially cosmetic.

Asian companies can be just as bad or even worse.

CCT Resources, a subsidiary of Hong Kong's CCT Telecom, spent $100 million in 2008 buying 300,000 hectares – an area five times the size of Hong Kong – of mostly virgin forest in Indonesia's remote Papua province. It announced it would be converting roughly two-thirds of it to growing palm oil and would start felling trees in 2009. Preposterously, the company claimed that replacing the forest with oil palms would benefit the environment – despite the well-documented fact that felling natural forest results in emissions of carbon and other greenhouse gases far in excess of any possible gains, even if the palm oil is used for biofuel.[9]

Profiles of CCT Resources' management team suggest a lack of both experience and concern for any sustainable approach to forestry or plantation operations, indicating instead a group of people heavily weighted toward telecommunications, electronics and technology. But it is not hard to see why the company would want to get its hands on this business. CCT Telecom's main business, in telecom products, has been struggling in recent years. Given that the revenues from the timber that comes from clearing the land to grow palm trees would bring in an estimated $150 million, even before selling a drop of palm oil, the project looks sure to be profitable.

For everyone else, this project looks terrible. Recent government policies promoting palm oil plantations are undoing much of the progress Indonesia had made in slowing deforestation rates. Instead of increasing the productivity of barren or unused land already stripped of trees, it is speeding up the clearing of virgin forests due to a lack of transparency and mismanagement of concessions – and because money can be made by selling the timber. According to a United Nations Environment Program report issued in 2009, if current trends continue, Indonesia's remaining rainforest will cover less than half the area it did in 1990 by 2030.[10]

In both these examples companies are responding to the markets, but the markets do not create the decentralized incentives to do the right thing as Krugman suggested – rather the opposite.

Letting 'Father Greed' run wild will not produce solutions to the impact of consumption on 'Mother Nature'; it will simply destroy it. This is not a case of finding the innovations that will reverse climate change or halt the over-exploitation of resources – it is a case of refusing to take such a route in the first place. Only the most naïve would expect the private sector to play the driving role in resolving the resource and environmental challenges that lie ahead.

Finance – business's great enabler

Finance is business's other great enabler, providing the means for companies to take an idea and develop it into a profitable product or service. Finance is intimately connected with both technology and markets. People dream that markets and technology will allow the world to find answers to its sustainability issues, so finance is seen as the facilitator that provides the funds that will make the development of such answers possible.

At the heart of finance is a search for market 'inefficiencies' – opportunities to make money by providing funding. This can be as simple as buying something that is priced low in one place but can be sold for more in another. Or it can involve offering finance to a business to fill an apparent market gap with a new product or service.

Perhaps even more than communications technology, finance lies at the heart of globalization – not just helping companies trade between different locations, but allowing them to set up and run operations thousands of miles from their home, where land, labour and resource costs are cheaper and regulatory regimes more lax.

But finance's ability to provide the funding for any business venture that can bring it an appropriate return is what makes it hugely problematic for the development of sustainable economies. Its sole mission is to come up with optimal financial returns; other matters need only be considered as far as they affect this goal. It is blind to the environmental or social impact of any project it funds.

It is also a major accelerator of business through its ability to extend loans and credit. An individual could save for five years, then buy a car, or drive it away today using financing. From the point of view of growth, the latter is a far superior choice: the maker of the car and the sales outlet can both register a sale while the bank gives out a loan on which it earns interest. The economy has just got bigger, and as petrol is consumed and spare parts bought, it continues to grow faster than if the car had not been bought for several years.

In the United States and other Western nations, financial institutions drove growth through the 1990s and 2000s by searching for every way they could to extend credit and invent new products. Consumption soared as consumers, especially Americans, borrowed money, took on mortgages they could not afford and then withdrew equity from properties they could not afford in the first place in order to consume more.

For sure, banks may be a little less willing to lend since 2008 – and consumers less likely to borrow – but finance, because of its role as an enabler, will always be an advocate of doing more business not less; of having greater, rather than more efficient, turnover. If property prices start rising again, then banks will once more encourage homeowners to remortgage their homes.

As with business, the financial industry finds it hard to be involved in projects centred on meeting basic needs due to its desire for short-term, platinum-plated solutions that either guarantee or have the prospect of high returns. Mergers and acquisitions are a favoured activity. Despite the long and well-documented history of most such deals destroying value rather than creating it, they are extremely profitable for banks, lawyers and other advisers involved.[11]

Finance is also partly responsible for the misplaced belief that there must be 'innovative technologies' awaiting discovery that can solve the world's climate and environmental problems. With funding from investment banks, private equity funds or venture capital all looking for opportunities to discover the next technological leap to a better world, incentives to retain or adopt more prosaic but less resource-intensive techniques, such as those involving traditional practices, are severely weakened.

And finally, of course, finance likes any business where it can trade financial instruments – hence its fondness for the leading financial innovation associated with the environment, the trading of emissions permits. Usually known as cap-and-trade, these schemes involve governments granting companies permits to emit a set amount of carbon. If they emit more, they have to buy further permits; if they emit less, then they can sell their excess capacity.

Superficially, this looks like a smart way of motivating companies to reduce their emissions. In practice, however, carbon trading has many drawbacks. Usually set up by banks, the schemes inherently favour big companies that have the ability to navigate their complex regulatory structures and practices. The benefits – in effect, subsidies – also flow largely to polluting companies. Communities or businesses already operating in carbon-free ways get nothing, and makers of renewable energy equipment find it harder to establish themselves and market their products. Existing polluters, such as large electricity generators, in contrast, have been practically handed rights to trade, typically at a discount and often for nothing. Under systems set up in Europe, some major emitters of greenhouse gases have earned windfall profits simply by selling the permits they were granted. Many offset credits bought from other countries, especially those in the developing world, in effect supplementing fossil fuel use rather than replacing it.

Then there is cheating – particularly concerning carbon offsets. Take the example of wind farms. Supposedly, subsidies are only supposed to be granted to wind farms that would not be built otherwise. Such an unverifiable system can easily result in a search for ways of playing the system. And it has: in 2009, the UN's organisation for overseeing carbon trading halted subsidies to Chinese wind farms because of suspicions of manipulation.[12]

Emissions trading is a distraction from the search for real solutions to climate change. It is a way of avoiding confronting the problem of environmental degradation. Naturally, banks (and economists) prefer schemes that include them to other measures, such as direct command and control systems in which governments set the level of emissions and then fine any companies that exceed it.

Ostensibly an attempt to reduce emissions, cap-and-trade has turned out to be a mechanism that promotes the interests of financial institutions – giving them another market to take advantage of. Financial institutions, with their track record of large pay packets and mismanagement, should be the last people given the responsibility for the future of the world. In the end, finance is an enabler of business, but it is also a major obstacle in the establishment of sustainable economies.

No technological panacea

But if markets and finance cannot save us by themselves, what of the possibility that human inventiveness can resolve our problems? Can people use ingenuity to come up with technological solutions smart enough to ensure we can have all the material and other goods we dream of without destroying the earth?

Thomas Friedman is far from the only person with such hopes. Bjørn Lomborg believes that the richer we get, the more likely we will be to come up with a suitable invention: 'Clearly we'll have more and more problems, as more and more [people] are going to be richer and richer, using more and more stuff. But smartness will outweigh the extra resource use.'[13]

Jeffrey Sachs sees the problem similarly: 'The current trajectory of human activity is not sustainable… Yet if we channel a modest part of our growing resources and knowledge into high-S[ustainable] technologies, the result can be very different.'[14] In short, although we don't have the answer, don't worry, something will probably turn up. No company CEO would depend on some undefined future development to safeguard the future of his or her business, and no competent board would allow it. Yet, serious opinion makers rely on this argument rather than face the uncomfortable truth.

That technology and its money-making potential can be combined to solve the biggest dilemma human beings have ever had to face is a nice idea. For its proponents it also has the appeal of buying in support from some of the biggest winners – and so the possessors of the biggest vested interests – of the last three decades, such as technology companies, those who financed them, and the stock markets on which they are listed. Such interests are, of course, very happy to claim they may well be able to find the solutions.

Conceptually, the problem such ideas run up against is that throughout history technology has accelerated resource depletion, not reduced it. Take felling trees. Until the Second World War this was largely done by hand. But advances in engineering driven by military needs for lighter engines and metals led to the development of small, reliable and powerful chainsaws. In the first half of the 1950s, these transformed the logging industry in North America. Within a decade, they had transformed the logging industry around the world. Literally overnight, lumberjacks found themselves able to cut down trees between a hundred and a thousand times faster than they could with axes. Tractors then sped up the removal of lumber from weeks to days, and helicopters have now cut it to hours.[15]

The impact of the chainsaw and the countless other examples of inventions that transformed people's ability to affect the world cannot be reversed by hoping that innovation will find better ways of doing things.

The evidence of the last two centuries is the opposite: that in consumption-driven capitalist societies technology will be applied to meet and expand consumption and the infrastructure that supports it. This is not to say that there are not technologies which, if made widely available, would help to make economies sustainable. But that is not where the priority is now – and nor is it where creative energy is being directed.

Worse still, technology has so far failed to make a meaningful difference in the one area that people such as Lomborg and Friedman hope it will be particularly effective: reversing climate change. The world continues to move in the wrong direction. Currently the concentration of carbon dioxide in the atmosphere stands at 400 parts per million, up from around 275 ppm before the time of the industrial revolution. According to the most recent assessment by the Intergovernmental Panel on Climate Change, keeping carbon dioxide levels to its suggested level of 450 ppm will mean reducing annual emissions of the gas to four billion tonnes by around 2050.

To do this would call for cutting emissions by just under 5 percent each year over the next four decades. But growth in both the world's population and its income are pushing emissions in the opposite direction. Tim Jackson, an economist specializing in sustainability issues, notes in *Prosperity Without Growth*, that if the world population rises to 9 billion by 2050, and annual income growth averages 1.4 percent, then global carbon intensity – the amount of carbon used per unit of economic output – would have to fall by 7 percent each year over the next four decades. That is ten times the average amount it has fallen since 1990.

Under these circumstances, to make sure the world did not exceed its 450 ppm carbon dioxide target by 2050 would mean cutting the average carbon content per unit of economic output to just one-twentieth of what it now is.[16] We do not have the technology to do this. Nor is it in the pipeline. All that we have is a hope that we might find it somewhere. For sure, there are technologies that may allow us to mitigate the resource depletion and environmental consequences we face, such as embarking on a massive nuclear power station construction programme. But such answers have their own hurdles to overcome, and pursuing them still fails to confront the issue that the demand for resources posed by the continued pursuit of consumption-driven capitalism is not just an energy issue, but an across the board demand that has already overstressed the environment on multiple fronts. As Asia continues its march down a consumption-driven route, its demand for resources and its impact on the environment can only accelerate. In these circumstances, saving resources is impossible. Even the most efficient techniques may not result in a slowing of the rate of growth.

But even these are unlikely to make much difference. Incremental improvements will not get us there. Combine the same scenario of a world population rising to nine billion with average annual income growth of 1.4 percent, and the same kind of fall in carbon intensity that we have managed in the last twenty years, and carbon emissions will be 80 percent greater in 2050 than they are now.

This and the other environmental issues we face are not matters that can be overcome by channelling a small part of the world's existing wealth into research and development and new technologies. Nor are they ones that can be resolved by a more efficient use of resources. They can only be seriously met by using less, and this requires a dramatic shift in the way we imagine – and plan for – the future.

Change must be confronted

Given the shortcomings of markets, technology and finance in offering the world a viable way forward through the twenty-first century, why is it that so many commentators like them?

For Thomas Friedman, a key reason is the impossibility of global cooperation: 'Anyone who watched the chaotic way this [Copenhagen] conference was "organized," and the bickering by delegates with which it finished, has to ask whether this 17-year UN process to build a global framework to roll back global warming is broken: too many countries – 193 – and too many moving parts.' And he is probably right. Given the total lack of progress since the Kyoto Protocol was adopted in 1997, and the failure of the Copenhagen climate summit, it is hard to see the world reaching a consensus on global warming, let alone the host of other issues it needs to address.

But there is also another explanation. Friedman's proposal, and those of Lomborg, Sachs and most other commentators, allows the world to continue as it is. Unless they want to, no one has to change, and no great vested interests need be attacked. Sacrifices, as I mentioned in the previous chapter, would not be required.

Unfortunately, we do not have the luxury of hoping that painless routes will get us where we want to go. We cannot have a world in which an ever-increasing number of people in Asia enjoy an ever-greater level of consumption while the world's innovators and inventors figure out how they can then be switched to doing this in an environmentally 'efficient' way. In the next few decades, financial markets will not figure out ways to reduce our carbon emissions by swapping permits to trade; technology will not have delivered a series of magic bullets allowing everyone to consume freely without considering their resource and environmental impact.

For humanity to find a way forward, change in the way societies act, therefore, must be accepted as inevitable. The world has reached a stage where economic growth, and in particular trying to maintain it via consumption-driven capitalism, has become the driver of our problems. The problems of resource depletion, pollution, environmental degradation and climate change are ones that in combination require us to step far beyond the framework of economics. Indeed, they can be in large part attributed to economists and the role they have played as agents of growth.

For Asia, poised as much of it is on the brink of consumption, the struggle to consider alternatives may be particularly difficult. But, paradoxically, by virtue of the consequences that would befall the region if it were to take this route, it has a greater need – and so potential – to rethink the future than any other part of the world.

Passenger car production
Millions

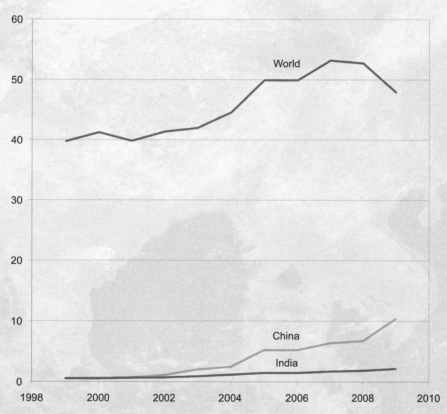

Source: International Organisation of Motor Vehicle Manufacturers

3
RETHINKING THE FUTURE IN ASIA

The countries of Asia must rethink their futures. Continuing down the road of consumption-driven capitalism is not an option, nor is hoping that markets, technology and finance will come up with a magical fix. As they rethink, many will find themselves having to challenge conventional economics and views about the role of the state. Moreover, they will discover that there is no 'one size fits all' solution; each country will have to come up with its own policies, tailored to its specific conditions and needs.

But there are some common themes that all responses will necessarily have to address in order to be effective. First is a rejection of the ways of thinking that have brought the world to its current precarious state. Second is replacing those approaches with new tools capable of handling the development problems countries face. And, finally, the third is setting new directions that allow countries to ensure futures that are equitable and sustainable.

This does not mean rejecting or trying to reverse the economic development of the last several decades, neither in the West nor in Asia. Indeed, growth has had a golden period and brought with it numerous benefits for a huge number of people around the world. But that era has ended. The golden period of growth was propelled by an ever-accelerating use of resources. We now know that this formula, while able to raise the standard of living for a sizeable minority of the world's population, does not – cannot – apply to the world as a whole.

Growth has to be redirected away from the resource-intensive path it has taken in the last two and a half centuries towards activities that offer all humans at least the same (and possibly greater) opportunities to flourish. We have to put limits on the use of limited resources. So as well as focusing on the quantity of consumption, we need to look at its quality – what consumption is composed of and what changes can be made to it.

The central subject of this chapter is the question of how Asian countries can rethink their patterns of development to ensure that the well-being of people alive now does not endanger the prospects of future generations.[1] To do this we must look at the values ignored or downplayed by conventional economics in order to, as environmental economist Clive Spash puts it, end the 'allegiance to an economic orthodoxy which perpetuates the dominant political myth that traditional economic growth can be both sustained and the answer to all our problems'.[2]

Rejection

The dominant economic orthodoxy has a strong hold over Asia. The practices and ideology of consumer-driven capitalism did not just mysteriously arrive in the region and naturally take root. Western companies and Western governments actively promoted them.

Much as the shape of the American financial system was determined by its banks and other institutions – which spent hundreds of millions of dollars on lobbying to free themselves of regulatory constraints – so across Asia, Western business interests and their Asian proxies have endlessly lobbied to be allowed to act as freely as possible. The World Bank and the World Trade Organization supported their efforts with missions and 'advisers' to governments along with report cards praising economies that had liberalized and criticizing backsliders.

Thus for decades governments have been told that the path to development lies through the establishment of market economies, open to trade with and investment from the rest of the world, with the rule of law protecting property and contracts, and – ideally – with democratic elections. The payoff, they were also told, would be worth it: not only stronger economic growth, but improved transparency and accountability, better governance, less corruption and greater individual freedom. In sum, not only could free markets help make everyone richer; they could also help them be better.

Rejecting such a powerful body of ideas and replacing it with new ways of thinking is not easy. Despite the very recent financial crisis, this ideology continues to dominate economic agendas around the world. But if Asian countries are to find a new direction for their societies and economies, they must move beyond these ideas. To do this, they must fully understand what it is in this ideology that has brought them to where they are now, and the assumptions upon which it is based.

The last chapter explored why markets cannot be expected to 'do the right thing' and solve global environmental and resource challenges. Here again, Paul Krugman offers a useful starting point towards developing a new set of principles. Economics' core insight, he says, is the efficiency markets bring to transactions between people: 'Free markets are "efficient" – which, in economics-speak as opposed to plain English, means that nobody can be made better off without making someone else worse off.'[3]

Implicit in this conception of efficiency is that everything works smoothly because of the freely made decisions of individuals. Governments should have no say in setting prices or allocating resources. Regulation, where it exists, should be as light as possible. Wherever possible, individuals should be free to choose and do what they want, according to their own needs and tastes. It is a beguiling and powerful proposition – not just because it promises to deliver the best economic results but because by doing so it also delivers a better society of greater freedom for all.

But it is also hugely problematic. Aside from its stress on individual rights, and total silence on those of the group, buried at its heart lies a notion of 'more' – not just that the total gains to producers and consumers are shared out in ways that leave everyone a little happier (the producer makes a profit while the consumer has a shiny new product or service), but that repeating and expanding this process with whatever inputs and materials there are at hand can produce ever-expanding amounts of 'more'.

This 'more' is what governments like. Despite the global financial crisis and the backlash against free markets it created, economics is still the place governments instinctively look to for solutions – even for a challenge as threatening as climate change – because of this beguiling promise of 'more'.

As we saw in the last chapter, most mainstream suggestions on how to confront environmental challenges use some combination of market-driven technological innovation and financial engineering for solutions centred on producing 'more'. But this search for more ignores the undue attention consumption-driven capitalism places on the present and on what people are doing now. An inevitable side effect of this myopic focus on the present is a lack of attention on the effect of today's decisions on the future.

This future impact fits nicely within Krugman's statement that markets are efficient because 'nobody can be made better off without making someone else worse off'. (There are no win-wins, only winners and losers.) Implicitly, the discussion here focuses on the present and what to do with all the things we have available to us now. But what if markets encourage more consumption now to benefit people today but, in doing so, deplete resources or have an environmental impact that will make future generations worse off?

Unfortunately, considering the dilemma of how today's consumption will impact future generations does not fit within the spectrum of economic thought. Economics focuses on short-term thinking, and here lies the biggest problem.

In effect, economics has created its own reality. Its model for the world – encouraging consumption in order to drive growth – has taken over. In Adam Smith's time, this was not so important. (Today's economists who seem to cite Smith all the time should note that he has been dead for over two hundred years.) When resources had barely been tapped and the number of people exploiting them was relatively small, consuming more to make more and raise standards of living made sense. Now, however, with the world already at its limits, this outlook is more than misguided, it is dangerous. Worse still, economics' attempts to get out of this problem could drive it over the brink.

Discounting the future

To think about how human activities affect the future, economists use what they call the 'social discount rate' – essentially how much people are prepared to spend (or forgo spending) now to prevent future damage. A high rate suggests that people are unconcerned about what the value of something will be in the future – they are more interested in what it is worth to them now. A low rate suggests the opposite – that they want the things available to them now also to be available to future generations.

In terms of resources – a forest, for example – a high discount rate would mean depleting it now and hoping that future generations have other ways to make money, possibly more fruitful ones created in part by investing the money made from selling the resource. A low discount rate, in contrast, might mean only felling trees at their replacement rate, and so passing the entire forest on intact to future generations.

Other things being equal, it is impossible to say which course of action is right. Felling the trees and reinvesting the money might lead to a sizeable increase in wealth that benefited both current and future generations. Harvesting the trees sustainably might leave both current and future generations poorer, but with a forest where they can relax and enjoy nature.

Research into attitudes and behaviour concerning discount rates reveals a contradiction. People say they favour a low discount rate, but their actions belie their words – or in other words, while they would like to do good things for the future, actually they prefer to consume now.

We should not be surprised by this. Various forces encourage faster rather than slower resource depletion. Most significantly, people value what they can consume now more than what they might be able to consume in the future. The one way they can be encouraged not to consume a resource now is if its future value is likely to be greater than exploiting it and investing the money; if its value were likely to grow more slowly, then they would be better off depleting it. Finally, people in the future have no say in setting the value of something now – regardless of how highly they might value it. Take these factors together, and we have what Jeffrey Sachs calls the 'tyranny of the present'.[4]

Some economists do not see this as a problem. They argue that we should not anticipate future challenges, such as climate change, and try to solve them now. Instead, we should realize as much growth as possible, because then future generations will be in a better position to solve such problems, especially as exactly what needs doing might be clearer.

Others take a less extreme view – but one rooted in the same logic. They conclude that the best approach is to spend a little money now but see this ramped up over time as future generations find themselves able to spend more.

What this amounts to, however, is cutting down the trees to fight climate change. The alternative – proposing that consumption be forgone – is hard for economists to justify. It means accepting that people should voluntarily remain poorer now than they would otherwise be, despite the likely outcome of future generations being better off. It also runs against economic logic that we should be maximizing market efficiency, underlining once again just how hard it is for economics to say stop.

Perhaps we should not be surprised. Economics, after all, is about identifying ways of generating growth. If we want something other than growth, then we should look elsewhere.

In most areas, this might be exactly what we would do. Given the weight given to economics in all areas of policy making, governments find it hard to accept that they should be considering alternatives. Nor is it surprising that other vested interests, business in particular, would want to foster such thinking. As we saw in the previous chapter, the goal of companies is to secure short-term gains for their owners. It is in their interests to offload costs and risks on to others. And what better 'other' to offload risks on to than a future that is unable to voice its opposition or even reservations? Politicians looking to be re-elected have similar short-term agendas, often merging with those of companies.

But as the inherent problems of the social discount rate demonstrate, flaws in economic theory have the potential to generate hugely negative impacts in the real world. If economics cannot come up with a credible way of thinking about the future, then we must abandon its planning tools. We know that continued growth in Asia will not create solutions to its environmental challenges; if economics cannot come up with a better answer then we must put the tools of economics aside and stop allowing economists to set the agenda.

Towards resource management

The conundrum we face is relatively simple to state: can Asia develop without resorting to the type of growth that destroys our planet? The answer requires an alternative that can relieve the region from the drive to consumption.

For the developed world, the problem revolves around restricting the growth of consumption, and making what consumption there is far more efficient in its use of resources, thereby restricting its environmental impact. Discussions on how this could be managed are taking place.[5] But because these are centred on how to meet the needs of rich countries, they are of little immediate relevance to Asia.

Across the region, hundreds of millions of people living in poverty face the problem of not having enough to consume. They cannot even consume basic necessities such as food, housing, sanitation, education and health care. These people need more investment, not less, so they can have access to such fundamental goods and services. Above them on the prosperity scale are those identified in the introduction as standing at the threshold of consumption. These people are not yet rich but are looking to improve their standards of living and enjoy lifestyles that people in developed countries have had for decades.

For all these people, running down resources is not an option. Nor is relying on such orthodoxies as 'market efficiency' to determine how best to maximize consumption. Instead, we must figure out ways in which we can use the limits imposed by resources and their environmental impact to direct sustainable development.

This requires putting the management of natural resources at the centre of everything that people do. Countries must move away from those conceptions of efficiency that economics has wielded so powerfully to exploit natural resources, and instead use the notion of limits to set a greater framework within which other tools – including markets – then do their work of securing the most efficient returns. Much work here will be concentrated on replacing an obsession with the level of consumption with a focus on the composition of consumption so that, even on a scale envisaged by Asia's population, the impact on the environment is manageable.

But before we move on to some practical rules for guiding societies towards making resource management central to their governance, we must first look further at the nature of the constraints that should be applied.

Risk minimization

Throughout this book, the word development has been preferred to growth as the goal governments should be striving to realize for their societies. This, however, should not be taken to imply a simple rejection of growth, but rather of its use as a shorthand for the stimulation of consumption. In itself, growth is neither good nor bad; it is the way in which it is achieved that can be problematic.

Applying the principle of using resource management to limit environmental impact is not to say that growth should be halted or reversed. Such simplistic solutions should be rejected.

While mainstream thinking turns to notions of markets, innovation and finance in search of solutions, too many among the 'green' brigade simply demand an immediate transformation of society. What is required are ideas that acknowledge the need for development, but which allow us to re-prioritize how that development is achieved in order for societies to arrive at an appropriate composition of consumption at the 'right' level.

True, for some resources such as rainforests, fisheries and various metals and minerals, the answers will necessarily require total or near total bans on exploitation. But on the broader canvas of a society's needs, such command and control solutions may be well intentioned but fail to take into account both people's needs and the many vested interests that are huge obstacles to change.

A useful framework for guiding our way forward can be found in the ideas of a different approach: risk minimization.[6] Risk minimization suggests that while the outcome we are looking for is the transformation of societies, we are more likely to achieve this objective by placing it within a framework aimed at multiple, much smaller, targets than by making wholesale change the principal goal. Particularly when presented with a large but uncertain threat that might affect many people in different ways, it may be better to look for measures that could moderate its impact rather than strive to realize a grand strategy that could totally prevent it. Certainly, not having a perfect solution should not prevent mitigating steps being taken, while avoiding sweeping immediate change is also less likely to stir up opposition or lead to other unanticipated problems.

In some ways, risk minimization would seem to overlap with the precautionary principle. The precautionary principle's great weakness, however, is that while it sounds like common sense, it offers little guidance on exactly what should be done to counter any particular perceived threat. In the face of climate change, for example, the precautionary principle says nothing more than that action should be taken to avert it. Risk minimization, in contrast, offers far greater potential for building consensus that results in real change. Its goal is less to find ultimate solutions than to try to identify ways of moving forward that would subsequently lower the need for more drastic actions.

We might, for example, say we want to transform the management of fisheries in Asia to make them sustainable. Laudable as such a goal is, it would instantly generate complaints from all the vested interests involved, making progress impossible and ending in no action being taken. A risk-minimization approach, in contrast, would aim to identify the biggest threats to fisheries and then try to address those, but at the same time would embrace smaller steps that might lead to its greater goals being reached. It would encourage countries to take action individually rather than looking for cross-border agreement. It might suggest the setting up of marine reserves, the funding of local eco-tourism projects, the use of quotas or the imposing of bans for part of the year, as China now does. Where economic returns were already low, it might offer compensation and proposals for alternative jobs.

Certainly, such an approach would still have to overcome vested interests, but it could weaken these by taking those steps which did not need consensus for action, or which were readily affordable. Of course, risk-minimization does not guarantee success, but it does allow governments to prepare the way for bigger action if it proves necessary later, while avoiding what may prove unnecessary expenditures along the way. It is suitable for countries at all levels of development within Asia. Moreover, it can be applied within any political system, from one-party states to fully fledged democracies, and can bring results regardless of the strength or weakness of a country's government.

Risk minimization may prove particularly useful in tackling climate change. Currently, even among those who accept that climate change is a real threat, there are huge differences of opinion on what action should be taken. Typically, stances on this spectrum of opinion are set by vested interests. Advocates of a 'big bang' approach to climate change, for example, are usually those who would lose little from drastic measures being adopted now. Resistance comes from those with high stakes in things as they are. The hope, of course, is that a global solution is found – possibly helped by a technological or engineering breakthrough. But with no such answer in sight, and continuing uncertainty over exactly what the ultimate outcome of climate change might be, most countries opt for inaction.

A risk-minimization approach would look to escape this impasse through a combination of taking action where it could be easily realized while looking for ways of mitigating what appeared to be the greatest danger. It would try to balance potential threats against current interests, and then push for change that reduced danger. Its acceptance of trade-offs might frustrate advocates of radical and immediate change, but need in no way compromise the greater goal of moving towards sustainable societies. Certainly, its approach does not rule out drastic action, but in looking to take such a course only in the face of clear-cut threats, it reduces the chances of governments having to attack entrenched interests without widespread support. It is particularly useful in trying to figure out ways of moving forward against multiple fronts and multiple forms of resistance to change.

As Vaclav Smil, a vehement advocate of risk minimization, points out, while the world depends on fossil fuels for energy, cutting emissions of greenhouse gases can be best realized through policies that encourage the lowest practicable energy flows. In itself, this would provide insurance against climate change. But this would only be one of its benefits. Arguably more important would be the reduced consumption of fossil fuels, which in turn would have multiple benefits, including less damage from mining, oil spills and acidification of oceans, and better air and improved health as fewer pollutants are released. In addition, any country that lowered its energy flows while producing the same level of economic activity would also improve its competitiveness, and so create more jobs.

Later, in the conclusion to this book, I address what specific policies countries can adopt to reach these goals. For now, I want to underline that, for Asian countries, adopting risk minimization as their core means that thinking about the future provides them with a tool to balance the interests of people alive today with those as yet unborn. We do not want to squander time, effort and resources on unnecessary actions, but we must take out insurance against an unpleasant future.

New tools

While resource management offers us a broader framework within which to operate, and risk minimization puts forward a general pragmatic approach to guide governments, we still need some practical maxims to determine what it is we should actually be doing.

The starting point for this has to be an awareness of the importance of gauging the resource and environmental constraints we face and what limits we should subject ourselves to. With this knowledge in place, we can determine the right level of consumption.

Asia must switch its priorities from the pursuit of growth to economic management based on sustaining its resources and productive bases over the long haul. Societies must also take action, looking at what and how much they consume. The key priority is determining how to use and manage the resources available to avert ecological disaster. The principal tool is the deployment of constraints. Both of these require a new mindset, one that abandons the belief that growth will lead to prosperity for all and accepts that much of the world's economic growth stems from being allowed to ignore the long-term costs of its environmental impact.

What is needed is *genuine investment* – investment that produces better outcomes over time when all costs are taken into account. Genuine investment has two sides. First, that it preserves, or better still enhances, the value of 'natural capital'.[7] Second, that it ensures resources are shared equitably – both over time, by allowing future generations access to them, and within societies, by ensuring that everyone has access to what they need to have flourishing lives.

To do this we have to reverse centuries of thinking. Human history, at least since the invention of agriculture, has been about losses of natural capital – be it fossil fuels, rainforests, fisheries, coral reefs, aquifers, or even land via desertification or flooding due to rising sea levels. Before the industrial revolution, the earth could readily bear these costs, so they were ignored.

Capitalism was able to ignore the issue of pricing these resources during its early days. It no longer has that luxury. Growth on the scale envisaged by Asia's development over the next few decades will lead to a loss of natural capital that will dwarf the losses seen in the West during the twentieth century, let alone what the entire world managed in the centuries before that. Governments must direct their attention to the management of resources in ways they have never attempted before. And they must ensure that the products of development are shared equitably.

No longer can development that rewards only a few be allowed. Trickle-down economics assumes that the better off can enjoy a surplus because, in time, others will also benefit. No longer can we tolerate a system that allows a few to claim a disproportionate share of resources on the basis of a false promise that others will also be able to claim a growing share of those same resources for themselves in the future. We simply do not have the luxury of condoning such a wasteful system. In Asia, because of the size of the populations concerned, development will have to be both environmentally sustainable *and* equitable – markets cannot be allowed to determine the distribution of wealth because of both the inequities they create and the waste they produce.

Managing resources can be done in various different ways. Obviously by reducing consumption, but also by investing in different ways of doing things – ones that use less resources, ones that use more people, ones that rework incentives. The core tenets of what actions should be taken can be summarized under three headings.

1) Resources are constrained; economic activity must be subservient to maintaining the vitality of resources

Obvious as this sounds, the simple fact of resource constraints continues to be ignored. Resource and environmental realities mean that anyone who suggests that everyone in Asia can have the same consumption-driven lifestyles of the rich countries is peddling a lie. The four billion Asians living today cannot; the five to six billion in 2050 – even less so.

As has already been noted, the Western model has been advanced as a universal solution for the world's ills. But its twin assumptions – first of limitless resources; second, that bringing such limitless resources into play would allow us to overcome any problems encountered along the way – are false. Resources are limited, and the way we are using them will guarantee catastrophe. Instead, economic activity must be subservient to the primary goal of maintaining the vitality of resources – even more so in Asia than in the rest of the world because of the size of its population and the already degraded nature of much of its resources.

Governments must always bear in mind that economics should be used as a tool to reach other goals, not as a goal-setting mechanism in its own right. Our priority is not efficient growth, but sustainable development secured through the imposition of constraints. We do not need to ignore the benefits of well-functioning markets; markets are efficient at allocating resources by balancing supply and demand. But governments must be clear about who is setting the priorities and the goals must be determined at the level of society, clarifying what demand is and what the priorities are in allocating resources. Governments, not markets, should do this.

2) Resource use must be equitable for current and future generations; collective welfare must take priority over individual rights

Demands for prosperity will have to be balanced against the requirements of social justice, much of which is linked to fair access to resources. Basic needs must be met first, underlining everyone's right to water, food, sanitation, housing, education and health care. Resources must be used in ways that serve the majority rather than in ways that benefit a rich minority. The falsity of market capitalism's claim that it leads to a trickle-down of wealth should be highlighted. (Distributing prosperity equitably by raising the living standard of the world's poorest people also has the benefit of lowering fertility rates, ultimately resulting in lower population growth and with it a lower demand on resources.[8])

3) Resources must be repriced; productivity efforts should be focused on resources, not people

Following from this, resources must be repriced. Wherever possible, market capitalism has deliberately downplayed or ignored negative external factors that would increase costs. This must be reversed.

Emissions must have costs attached to them. Other resources – especially land and water – must have prices that compel people to use them in a sustainable fashion. Where necessary, outright bans must be placed on the use of particular resources, for example, rainforests and fisheries threatened by depletion.

The emphasis on raising labour productivity that has dominated industry since the onset of the industrial revolution should be replaced with an emphasis on raising resource productivity. Governments should encourage innovations that use fewer resources rather than fewer people, particularly when it comes to land use and water. Raising the prices of natural inputs would help here, as would removing or lowering income taxes. (Farming is an area where such changes could reap huge benefits by removing the subsidies now supporting large-scale, input-intensive agro-industry and replacing it with labour intensive, chemical- and carbon-free farming.)

Are these tenets idealistic? No. Many of them already exist in one form or another. In recent years, China's leaders have been promoting the notion of a 'harmonious society' rather than the pursuit of growth at all costs that was the mantra of its previous leadership team. Throughout its economic take-off, Japan successfully shared its wealth equitably, avoiding the huge disparities in earnings of the United States. India is far better positioned to continue with labour-intensive farming than to push hundreds of millions of people from the countryside into cities. In Indonesia, relatively small revaluations of rainforest would be an enormous incentive for communities to develop businesses centred around caring for trees and their products rather than felling them.

Moreover, not only are these tenets perfectly applicable in practice – and in this book's conclusion, I discuss policies drawn from these tenets that governments should be considering – but I would also suggest that at the same time as governments in Asia identify those parts of Western economic and political orthodoxy that do not work for them, they should also be drawing strength from the fact that despite the relentless onslaught of market fundamentalists, they have all, albeit to varying degrees, resisted market capitalism's consumption-driven model. China has kept the core of its economy under state control. Japan, South Korea and Taiwan have maintained significant trade barriers. Many Indians, especially among the poor and tribal people, as one recent commentator notes, 'view globalization largely as a source of intrusion, dispossession and pollution'.[9]

As a part of the rethinking process, governments in Asia should study the ways in which the widespread application of market capitalism has undermined many of the traditional values that have served their societies for centuries if not millennia – in particular, by encouraging people to treat the world with disdain. In this they will be tapping into a rich vein. Many people in Asia lament the disappearance of age-old values – not that Asia is unique in this regard, but its hugely diverse range of cultures has already begun to disappear into a homogenized 'one world' culture of instant online or broadcast access to a handful of Western-originated tastes in media, food, sport and lifestyles.

What governments must do is include this discontent as part of their approach to reshaping people's expectations so that aspirations are aligned with constraints. The message they must deliver is that people should continue to aspire to be prosperous, but that their expectations must be aligned with the constraints under which all societies will have to operate – Asian ones above all. This does not mean that people cannot aspire to prosperity, still less that they will remain poor. But it does mean a rethink of the future beyond the bland assumptions of affluence that have been peddled across the region.

This rethink will include the creation of better references for people to measure their personal well-being against. As I discuss further, in the conclusion, measures could include restrictions on advertising that promotes resource-intensive goods or lifestyles, but could also be extended to the portrayal of groups beyond a person's immediate surroundings.[10] In 1999, Bhutan became the last country in the world to introduce television; a rise in crime since then has been widely attributed to young people being exposed to portrayals of Western consumption-filled lifestyles.[11]

This is not to suggest that governments restrict all access to information – a task that is all but impossible nowadays. But a switch of mindset towards constraining consumption could result in measures such as high taxes on advertising, strict controls on promotions aimed at children or creating an awareness of the need to restrain resource use a key part of education at all levels.

Countries in Asia need to come up with their own solutions, drawing on their respective indigenous strengths and borrowing from abroad where there are benefits in doing so. They need to look more towards their own forms of state. They will have to look at the values they must develop and protect. But they must also be states that can deliver what is needed and that, if they are to slough off the distortions of consumption-driven capitalism, will have to develop their own characters and not rely on being pale imitations of Western states.

Fish caught
Million tonnes

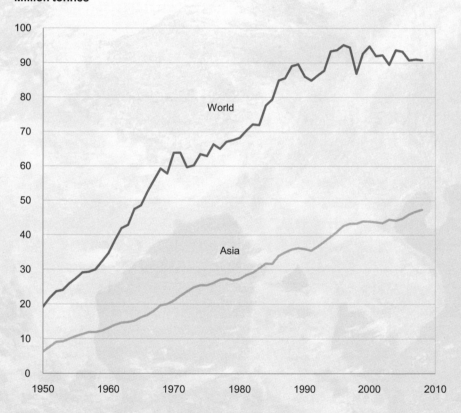

Source: Food and Agriculture Organisation of the United Nations

4

THE ASIAN STATE

I f Asia is to make the management of resources and their impact on the environment and societies the defining purpose of its governance, it needs strong states. The decades during which it was widely accepted that markets were the main deciding factor of the future of societies must be relegated to the past. Instead, we must accept that it is impossible to conceive of a society in which governments ignore the management of the natural goods and services their people will need to survive and thrive. The sheer number of people living in Asia and the point of development at which they stand make this management a priority. Countries across the region must recognize that if they are to succeed in establishing sustainable societies, powerful governments are key. They are the only institutions with the abilities and powers to deliver development while reversing environmental degradation, preventing resource depletion and maintaining social cohesion.

It is imperative, therefore, that nations strengthen their governmental capabilities in order to have the tools and capacities necessary both to address environmental resource issues and overcome resistance to change from vested interests, domestic and international. Instead of thinking about growth and development in terms of opening their economies and encouraging consumption, they must focus on finding economic tools that nurture their resource and environmental bases so that well-being can be shared equitably by current and future populations. Because of the specific nature of the challenges facing Asia, its nations will have to develop their own distinctive forms of the state. The next chapter considers the policy decisions states will have to make. This chapter examines the form states in Asia must take to generate and implement sustainable policies to meet future needs.

What should states be doing?

During the era of market fundamentalism, governments in Asia were repeatedly told by advocates of the Washington consensus that their job was to get out of the way. For sure, they had a handful of important tasks, including ensuring national security and providing basic legal, social and physical infrastructure, but otherwise the best thing they could do was interfere as little as possible, especially in the workings of the market.

That era looked like it came to a close with the global financial crisis. In its wake there have been vocal calls for much stronger government oversight of financial markets. As the financial crisis unfolded, it seemed the world was being presented with a chance to reassess both the mechanisms that had got it into such a terrible mess and the direction to follow as it entered the second decade of the twenty-first century.

BP's spillage of millions of barrels of crude oil into the Gulf of Mexico in 2010 led to further calls for tighter government monitoring of business. But despite the anti-market backlash, few steps have been taken to rework matters. Within months of the collapse of Lehman Brothers and the bailouts of Citigroup and American International Group, it was apparent that regulators in the United States and Europe were looking for nothing more than ways of making their financial systems less susceptible to shocks. The eventual US reforms, signed into law in the summer of 2010, were essentially a piece of housekeeping – major housekeeping, but not one that signalled a change in the way financial markets operate. In other words, the status quo continued.

Countries in Asia cannot follow a similar path. They have to draw far stronger conclusions from the events of 2008 than were drawn in America and Europe – above all, that the state must play a far greater role in the management of the economy if it is to ensure both current and future populations have adequate access to the resources they need. To guarantee this, the central duty of the state must be recast – from protecting individuals and their property to protecting natural capital and ecological services. If the state is to realize all these public interventions via the production and implementation of environmentally sustainable policies, the environment has to be put at the centre of policy making and not viewed as an adjunct to be considered in the making of other policies.

In most countries, environmental issues – including climate change – remain in the domain of environmental ministries. Rarely do environment regulators have any real power, despite a common acknowledgement that other ministries must take account of the environmental and climate impact of the activities under their jurisdiction, particularly in the areas of economic, energy, trade and transport policies. The World Bank notes: 'Environment agencies are normally weaker than departments such as treasury, commerce, or economic development. They tend to have fewer resources and to be represented in cabinets by junior politicians.'[1]

Such attitudes must be cast aside. Instead our natural environment must be made a foundation issue. It is, after all, the source of all wealth and well-being. The objective is not making governments, and through them the companies and individuals they govern, more responsive to environmental needs. It is to put the requirements of the environment and the resources it provides people with at the very heart of what governments do.

The last chapter argued that countries must find new ways of thinking that allow them to change direction, and proposed that this could be done by replacing traditional concerns with a new priority – putting resource management at the centre of policy making. This does not mean they should be trying to wind back the clock. The back-to-the-earth calls of those such as respected Indian ecologist Vandana Shiva are not the answer,[2] even though many current land use and farming techniques require changing. Incentives need to be devised that encourage small-scale food production, principally aimed at supplying local markets. At the same time, governments must inhibit the activities of multinational agri-businesses that work against such farming practices and ways of life.

But countries must start from where they are now. Nowhere are governments going to reverse the development Asia has gone through in the last several decades – nor should they try. From Japan through the tiger economies of east Asia, in large parts of south-east Asia, in China and in India, countries have realized development on a scale and of a nature that cannot be wished away or reversed. These national realities must be borne in mind when considering the possible ways of reacting to resource and environmental challenges.

Across Asia, states will have to develop a refined ability to manage their populations, particularly when it comes to shaping urbanization. Two countries which will have to wrestle with this issue are India, with nearly 700 million people still living in the countryside, and China, with around 500 million still in rural areas despite its rapid rate of urbanization. Despite having very different political structures, both India and China highlight the need for states that are strong and engaged. In both, governments will have to be involved in decisions determining the shape of towns and cities, and their links with the surrounding countryside, in ways that have never been seen before. They will have to integrate food and water supply networks, and share energy, transport and other resource systems. These are not responsibilities that can be left to markets or hands-off governments.

If China and India are going to achieve a balanced development path – as opposed to one driven by consumption economics – that allows them to manage environmental degradation while focusing on alleviating poverty, the state will have to play a major role. To some degree this is already happening, particularly in China.

Already, the Indian state is facing growing unrest in rural and tribal areas – the Naxalite movement is one example – as more and more communities feel a sense of loss. Hope is vanishing, even as the economy grows and their resources are usurped to meet the needs of the urban consuming classes. A future India that embraces more inclusive growth can emerge if it takes a different path that draws on the best of its rich traditions and customs. This does not mean that India simply reverts to its former, ill-conceived socialist habits, but it must look for ways of creating a different prosperity, one that is not based on consumption-led growth.

In this, it will need to find more subtle tools than China; its democratic nature bars it from the direct controls that can be brought to bear by Beijing. But rather than preventing India from using the various tools described in this book, democracy will force it to look for ways in which popular participation can be turned into an asset. What might concentrate minds is the lack of resources per head of population compared even with China, and the fact that much of its mineral wealth is located in its poorest regions, which are also the main centres of rural unrest.

For India to develop it will have to confront resource issues; opting to allow markets to be the deciding force in their exploitation will almost certainly result in major conflicts with tribal groups and accelerated depletion of already scarce resources. Such are their scales, and such the already precarious natures of their environments, that neither China nor India can maintain a growth-based approach to development, in the hope that ways of negating the environmental impact of their growth will be conjured up later.

As both India and China demonstrate, states must take the lead in two areas. First, they must concentrate on longer- rather than shorter-term development. As the last chapter showed, the tyranny of the present means that markets heavily discount the future. While it is important that government policy accounts for the immediate needs of the poorest and others who need support today, public policy must also take a much longer view of how benefits will be accrued and shared than markets do. Second, states need robust policies that unambiguously constrain resource use and consumption. These must give environmental factors and services realistic prices, and raise the value of natural capital. Rules must be put in place that restrict technologies, innovation and practices which encourage consumption, and which instead encourage investment in goods and services that reduce resource use. The specificities of what should shape such rules are the subject of the next chapter.

There is a third area states must consider. At least for the next five to ten years, national action is likely to prove more important than global action on a range of key environmental issues, including climate change. At first this might appear counter-intuitive. As the impact of climate change is global, it is almost universally argued that tackling it requires an international response, even if it is also acknowledged that because of the huge range and number of interests involved, putting together such a global framework will take time.

However, the search for such a global consensus is likely to prove futile in the next few years. There are simply too many conflicting interests between countries to expect any form of binding agreement with substantive measures to be reached in the time that is needed. Additionally, the search for such a consensus relieves countries of much of the pressure to do anything immediately because they offer the prospect of a better solution being found in the future.

Therefore, given the pressing nature of the challenges faced, Asian countries – especially the larger ones – are better off working within the risk-minimization framework outlined in the last chapter to devise policies and programmes that suit them and their particular needs. Of course, many environmental issues are cross-border and will need international or regional agreements at some point, but both China and India would do better to focus on resolving their internal energy, water and land issues than trying to reach agreements with the rich countries. What they, and the other nations of Asia, should focus on over the next decade is determining their own measures for managing resource and environment issues. Much of the detail – possibly most – will be decided by their specific social, political, cultural and economic conditions.

International agreements will also be necessary, especially where resources are used across borders – such as water originating in the Himalayas and many fish stocks. A host of issues will also require international agreement and cooperation because their impact is universal, most prominently climate change. But maintaining an ability to act freely will be vital for resource and environmental services management. This is because all action will, of necessity, be undertaken at a national level as the solutions which countries must come up with will essentially be local ones, ones that work within their own societies, not ones that are imposed on them from outside.

All this is in strict contrast to the notion generally advanced that what we need is more cooperation between countries. It also goes against the arguments made repeatedly through the 1990s and early 2000s that globalization was inevitably leading to a world where nation states counted for less.

Since the end of the 1980s, countries have repeatedly been told that they must open their borders and become more like each other if they are not to be left behind. Such calls, however, were those of market ideologists looking to advance the interests of the rich countries in general and the United States in particular. These forces are also likely to be a key element in resisting the imposition of real costs on resources and environmental factors that are currently excluded from the price of goods. At least in this respect, the world's financial crisis did everyone a favour, as rather than leading to more cooperation between nations it resulted in a strengthening of the role of sovereign states.[3]

Consequently, national-level action is far more important, and can bring major results. What we need are governments that see how it is in their best interests to act now rather than later, and understand that acting unilaterally is just fine. Indeed, successful unilateral results may even pave the way for subsequent international agreements. Thus, paradoxically, once these countries have figured out their internal resource and environment management systems, they will be in a better place to reach international agreements. This theme is explored further in Chapter 6.

It is more important that countries face inward and attend to domestic needs than it is that they face outwards, trying to coordinate their responses with other nations. And, at the national level, policies are needed to address crucial resource and environmental issues that can be sensibly tackled within a country's borders. The risk-minimization approach described in the previous chapter should offer almost every nation a range of measures that could be instantly and usefully adopted.

Handling this will be a tall order, requiring that states be both stronger and more independent than they have been in most countries across Asia. Countries, particularly the smaller and medium-sized ones, are likely to come under strong pressure from the rich countries, especially if their actions are taken to challenge the rules of Western-led international bodies such as the World Trade Organization.

Nonetheless, it is noteworthy that countries which have been able to resist such calls have done better at protecting national practices in business and other spheres from being overrun. Japan, for example, has managed to stall various efforts to open its markets to US businesses in a range of fields, from agriculture to construction. China, likewise, has maintained many barriers against penetration of its economy by forces it deems unwanted. Although it has opened many sectors, China has kept those industries it believes to be strategic off limits or heavily restricted – among them energy and resources, telecommunications services, and finance and banking.

Interventionist frameworks

What states must do is construct a framework of rules for their national economies with the management of resources and their environmental impact at the core. The principal tasks of these rules will be to ensure resources are used in environmentally sustainable ways, and that previously ignored or under-priced environmental factors are included in the costs of goods and services. They will also have to be enacted and executed in ways that receive popular support, ensuring that well-being is brought to all and shared equitably, and that expectations are managed in ways that restrain consumption.

States will need to be unashamedly interventionist. This should not be seen as outrageously controversial. The World Bank has noted: 'Climate change requires public interventions to address the multiple market failures driving it – the failures of pricing; of research and technology development; and of coordination and collective action, global, national, and local. As providers of public goods and correctors of externalities, governments are expected to address these market failures.'[4]

Or, put slightly differently, governments will have to live up to their responsibilities as the primary force overseeing the management of society. They will have to set the limits within which the private sector is free to operate and then ensure that these limits are respected. They will have to decide what measures should be used to mitigate the environmental impact of human activity, and then how such measures are communicated, regulated and enforced. Community involvement in all this will be vital, as will determining the appropriate degree of central oversight and decentralized day-to-day management.

Property rights

In particular, property rights and the enforcement of contracts will remain vital to the well-being of any society. One area that could be usefully explored by many countries is the power of the state to bestow property rights, possibly for a limited amount of time. This would be in contrast to the current Western-based thinking that emphasizes the state's role as the protector of property rights. Ownership rights could also be balanced with a greater emphasis on the duties and responsibilities that property brings with it – in particular, that usage rights must be tied to the responsibility of establishing and maintaining sustainable economies so they cannot be used in ways which deplete resources, pollute or emit greenhouse gases. Owners of land, for example, should be barred from over-exploiting or polluting it in ways that would reduce its value for future generations, particularly in their use of water and chemical fertilizers. The recent practice of states adopting licensing rights to public commons such as the radio frequency spectrum or the operation of mobile phone services could be extended to other areas, such as land and water. Mining concessions are already often managed in this way, but could be extended to include far greater responsibilities for the management of minerals and metals at the end of their life cycle.

Property rights will often have to be subordinated to usage responsibilities. Car owners, for example, cannot expect to have rights over the majority when it comes to the impact of their activities on air quality, carbon dioxide emissions, congestion, land uptake or noise pollution. There are also likely to be more situations where group rights must take priority over individual rights, notably in the use of commons. Land, water and mining resources are perhaps the biggest example: collective management of water resources is certain to be of vital importance across huge swathes of Asia.

For most countries, imposing 'capitalist'-style rights, especially through practices such as privatization, would rarely be the most appropriate option. Wherever possible, government should tap into traditions of collective management that have track records of sustainable management of resources. And governments must reverse the tendency towards an exclusive reliance on capitalist property rights. As William Easterly has pointed out, doing so often replaces traditional arrangements that played a major role in managing the difficulties of shared commons.[5] Often capitalist-style rights are introduced to facilitate transfers of ownership of land or resources to a company or individual better able to exploit them immediately for short-term gain, as has been the case with so many tracts of rainforest in Indonesia and other countries of south-east Asia.

For the poorest, however, Hernando de Soto's call for billions of poor people around the world to be given title to property they use or occupy but do not legally own should be heeded. Doing so could help an enormous number of people find their own means of development. India and Indonesia, with their large rural populations securing livelihoods from small-scale farming and forestry, would be particularly appropriate places for such practices, which could at the same time be targeted at reducing tree felling or mineral extraction by large domestic or multinational companies.[6]

Research and development, and education

Research and development will be an area where governments must concentrate more resources. It will be important that R&D is not directed principally at technology, as most officials tend to think it should be, but towards a far broader range of issues: what forms of social organization would best encourage reduced consumption; how depleted natural systems could be restored; how productivity could be focused on lowering resource usage rather than raising throughput volumes; what sort of educational and health care services would bring the best social returns – and so on.

Education will be a particularly important area for R&D. Governments will have to foster knowledge and awareness across societies, and oversee a range of transformations in outlook well beyond such obvious areas as building codes and energy efficiency – taking in matters such as reworking consumer organizations into consumption bodies, rewriting advertising standards and looking at the emphasis of civics courses in schools.

Redefining the state

The state that emerges from this process will be different from those we have seen in the past. It will be a state that accepts responsibility for environmental management; protecting resources and mitigating climate change will be its policy priorities. It will be a state that acknowledges that if it gets things wrong in these areas then the costs will far outweigh what it must spend now and in the coming years. But more than this, the state's key role will have been redefincd. It will be a state that ensures the well-being of its citizens by protecting the resources they need to live instead of just protecting their lives and property.

Will this lead to the return of big government? Bigger is not the issue or criterion here. Naturally, governments will have greater duties because they will also have greater responsibilities, and so will have to be involved in monitoring and restricting an enormous range of activities. Governments may get bigger, but they will also have to get better.

It is hard to envisage these states not being heavily involved in spending. Climate change mitigation and adaptation will almost certainly demand more government spending. If projections of more extreme weather events prove correct, then states will inevitably find themselves having to take care of more insurance, especially for those segments of the population unable to afford what are likely to be ever-increasing premiums. But as is explored in more detail in the following chapter, tax reforms are likely to be based around increasing rates sharply on resources and emissions while lowering them on income, especially for those on lower wages.

In Asia, Singapore already broadly embraces such a model with its Central Provident Fund. Scandinavian countries, with their high-tax and high-benefit regimes, are also likely to be useful examples. Asian countries could experiment with resource taxes aimed specifically at tackling poverty and environmental issues.

However, none of this signals a return to planned economies. States will subject their economies to far greater oversight in the use of resources. They will use taxes to reduce carbon and other greenhouse gas emissions, but also as a disincentive for other resource-intensive activities. They will have measures to encourage labour-intensive work. These new states will be active states, but active in the sense of setting frameworks of rules in which companies and individuals act, and then overseeing their implementation and enforcement. Their policies will be ones that encourage rising prosperity and people flourishing, but within a very different framework from that which has existed until now.

How to get the right kind of state

A prerequisite for strengthening environmental management is the building of stronger, more effective government institutions. How can this be achieved in ways that will ensure states in Asia produce the 'right' policies?

Obviously, it is hard for governments to strengthen themselves. But if they can reject the notion thrust upon them by pro-market demagogues over the last three decades that 'government is the problem, not the answer', they will be in a position to start looking at what interventions they should be making and what is the best way of going about it.

The state will have to strengthen its ability to resist claims by vested interests aimed at favouring their short-term needs at the longer-term expense of current and future generations. For many governments, this will be the hardest thing to do. The best way for them to do this will be to argue that what they are doing is necessary (no alternative) and equitable (shared fairly and in the best interests of all).

There are models out there. Both Singapore and Japan should be looked at for what they have achieved and how they have achieved it. Both have, to a greater and lesser extent, used the tools of 'guided' capitalism supported by a rule of law.[7] Despite having free elections, both have been for most of their recent history (all, in Singapore's case) 'one-party' democracies.

Governments can also highlight the problems developed nations have encountered with the growing power of lobby groups. In the US, in particular, politicians have largely abandoned the notion of acting for the public good to work instead as agents advancing the narrow interests of business and other constituencies with the financial power necessary to fund election campaigns.

States will not have to be perfect before they start acting. If the general principal of putting resource management at the centre of policy making is adopted, then even relatively weak governments can start with relatively small steps and aim to build their capacity over time.

It would be impossible, for example, for a country such as Indonesia simply to decide overnight that it was going to get tough with the huge range of vested interests currently attempting to exploit its forests. Currently, however, it has to try to reconcile the contradictory position of wanting both fast-track economic growth and the conservation of its natural resources. Given the dominance of market ideology, the former generally trumps the latter.

A lot of measures are simply about raising the level of implementation of existing practices, where doing so could save money or prevent wastage. Thailand, for example, has experimented with funding village-level business projects aimed at encouraging greater local self-sufficiency. Many of these schemes, however, have foundered on the mismatch between the time needed to get a project up and running and the time in which officials have to spend their budgets. Officials are judged on their ability to spend money within a financial year, not on whether the project they spend it on is successful. As many projects may take more than a year to introduce to villagers and be implemented, officials often simply hand over the money and move on. As a result, a lot of projects fail and much money is wasted.

Tackling this problem requires innovation, but not of the technological kind. Instead it requires three government organizations – the Budget Office, the Comptroller-General's Department and the Civil Service Commission – to find a new way of working together that ensures villagers get both the funding and the support they need.

Of course, just because a government puts resource management at the top of its priorities does not mean problems are solved automatically. But establishing it as the framework through which solutions are sought gives officials a different benchmark from the growth and financial targets they typically work under. Establishing a foundation of such practices, however weak initially, at least gives officials a base from which to start nibbling away at the power of vested interests. Especially important would be the grounds they would have for resisting claims by corporate interests that specific policies are anti-growth, because growth alone would no longer be the priority.

Would growth be slower? Possibly, but with the reorientation of national objectives away from growth to sustainability, governments would be able to deploy the argument that what they were guaranteeing was long-term growth for all, not just the minority which has typically tended to benefit.

Of course, none of this is easy. But nor is it utopian. Governments have pragmatic reasons for abandoning consumption-driven growth. They need to find these reasons and generate support for them. There will be opposition to such a change of direction, particularly from those who benefit from current ways of doing business, but this opposition has to be overcome, not surrendered to.

An authoritarian future?

Clearly the state must have the powers it needs to achieve the ends it wants. But this does not mean it has to be authoritarian. In general, it will help enormously if its population supports its actions. Governments will have an easier task if they make it clear they are intervening to protect the public good. And in this it will be beneficial for them to be both transparent and accountable.

Given the nature of the challenges facing Asia, it is important to figure out whether particular countries would be helped or hindered by democracy. Less important than the specific form of their political systems is whether they have the institutional structures to generate and implement policies that can realize the changes necessary in resource and environmental management.

In this respect, the question is not whether democracy is a good thing or not, but whether being a democracy helps a country develop and do what is necessary to adapt to or mitigate the resource and environmental constraints it faces. As Peter Burnell puts it:

...while in general democracies may be committed to protecting the people from undue harm this does not mean they all have the ability to do so. Nor does it mean that non-democracies must compare unfavourably. Almost regardless of the political regime and especially where the state is weak, establishing the managerial and organizational infrastructure and the economic and financial means to counter the damaging effects of climate instability could mean that democratic advance must take a back seat in some places.[8]

Such views, while acknowledging that Asia clearly needs more good governance, also suggest that good governance can be delivered by means other than the same package of beliefs advocated by Western liberal democracies. This is particularly true when it comes to emphasizing individual rights over collective rights and the pre-eminence of property rights in which Western capitalism is grounded. Indeed governments should tap into the growing feeling in many parts of Asia that there is a fundamental difference between democracy and good governance.

For the last few decades, under the convergence theory of globalization, countries have repeatedly been told that there is only one viable model, that of Western democratic capitalism. Rich countries developed the widespread conviction that their success could largely be attributed to a superior set of cultural and social values rooted in individual rights and linked to notions of democracy.

Of course, there has been resistance to this notion, particularly through the 1990s, in the promotion of the idea of Asian values. One particular example is China's long-maintained belief that it is developing its own brand of socialism with Chinese characteristics. Countries across Asia must reject the notion that the West has a 'package' of ideas and values that have to be applied as a whole – that it is not just markets, but markets plus liberal democracy – that somehow delivers the goods.

There can be no doubt that the world's richest countries are democracies. However, it is far less clear whether being democratic helps a country prosper or whether countries move towards democracy once their prosperity is assured.

It is hard to argue that its form of democracy has advanced the economy of the Philippines, or that Singapore's development has been held back by the way in which the People's Action Party has ruled uninterrupted since the city-state's independence in 1965. Likewise, India's form of democracy was widely regarded as being a key factor in retarding its development until the country's economic growth rate jumped to near-Chinese levels in the mid-2000s.

In the West, there has been a tendency to equate development and good governance with democracy. In many cases, however, the democractization of poorer countries has more to do with opening their markets than ensuring freedom for their populations. There is plenty of evidence that democratization, while leading to greater economic freedom, also results in a quicker and greater exploitation of resources, not necessarily to the benefit of the local population.

Recent events in Mongolia highlight how markets and resources can transform countries without leading to outcomes that benefit many people. International mining companies are lining up to exploit the country's mineral resources. Canada's Ivanhoe Mines and Anglo-Australian Rio Tinto have a multi-decade agreement to extract copper from the South Gobi. Total investment could reach $4 billion, equal to the country's total GDP in 2009. In the south of the country, China has invested $700 million to secure coal and other resources for its economy, while Mongolia's former colonizer, Russia, has mining interests in the north. With all this investment arriving, a range of forecasters, including the International Monetary Fund, are predicting that Mongolia will be among the top four fastest-growing economies in the world over the next decade.

But who will benefit? Ordinary Mongolians are struggling to survive. A harsh winter followed by a drought killed around ten million head of livestock in 2010, a fifth of the country's total. Older means of support, such as the collective farms of the Soviet era that ensured meat and other products could always be bought at a fixed price, have long since disappeared. Hundreds of thousands of Mongolians have left the countryside to move to the capital, Ulan Batur. There they join more than a million other Mongolians who have migrated to the city and live in tent districts, and who account for some 60 percent of the capital's population.

Two decades of market capitalism has brought Mongolia an internal refugee problem, the abandonment of lifestyles practised for centuries, and prospects – for a very few – of working for a foreign company. The nomadic way of life is hard. But what has replaced it has yet to offer any significant improvement for the vast majority of the population, despite having had a generation to do so.[9]

This example also highlights one other important value that is woefully underplayed by governments focusing on growth over social cohesion. Mongolia's socialist-era practices may not have resulted in prosperity, but at least they guaranteed that everyone was part of a social network. The market practices introduced by democracy have led to the demise of this network, explaining why when anyone's way of life collapses, due to bad weather or any other cause, their only option is to transport their family tent to Ulan Batur.

Other countries have fared much better in this respect. The relationship between Japan's government and society has been based on nurturing social cohesion, with links between officials, companies and society sustained by intricate networks of trust and support. The notion of the 'job for life' may have weakened in the last two decades, but the underlying belief in a more or less egalitarian society has been one of the key reasons for Japan keeping its unemployment rate so low since its 'bubble economy' ended in 1991.

Since its founding in 1965, Singapore has been a society dominated and directed by the state with the active support of its citizenry, despite government policies that would be politically unpopular in many other countries.[10]

Since abandoning central planning, China has developed its own version of a state-centric society supported by vigorous private and semi-private enterprise. Its lukewarm protection of property rights and legal recourse is little different from conditions in the imperial regimes that ran the country for millennia. The demise of its socialist healthcare and other services in the 1990s and early 2000s led to widespread comment that the country's adoption of market forces had, as in Mongolia, also led to a weakening of various social values. The goal of making China a 'harmonious society', unveiled by communist party leader Hu Jintao and premier Wen Jiabao in 2005, is in part an effort to rectify such failings by switching the previous emphasis on growth to establishing a more rounded and balanced society.

India, despite its democratic superstructure, has largely retained its traditional social organization. Looking at other countries across the region would reveal the same findings: that the countries of Asia, despite their exposure to global ideas and economics, have not seen their political forms converge with those of the West.

Of course, all these societies have absorbed practices from other countries – such as constitutions, elections, parliaments and Western-style militaries, to name just a few – but none has become a Western nation. (Japan, despite being the most developed, is arguably among the least influenced.)

Now they must formally recognise that the Western state model is not appropriate for their needs as the constituent parts of twenty-first-century

Asia. They must draw on their traditions, they must strengthen their moral authority, and use this as the basis to transform themselves into forces which can put the management of resources at the centre of their efforts to ensure viable, sustainable societies.

Ethical states

Under traditional conceptions of liberal democracy, the role of the state is to protect people and their property. Ostensibly, this role is neutral: it says little about how people act and what they do with their property. In the last thirty years, free market capitalism took this conception and used it to argue that the state should do the bare minimum – leaving people free to pursue their own interests – and that by doing so it would create the best conditions for economic growth.

In some ways it achieved its goal. Across Asia, governments discovered that freeing-up markets helped generate greater economic output. But this growth has come with severe environmental and resource degradation, most of which can be attributed to the underpricing of resources and ecological services. These costs must be priced in, and the only institution that can do this is the state.

Committing to do this, and protecting the well-being of today's populations and future generations, is a deeply ethical step. The importance of such a change cannot be underestimated. The way most governments have operated in recent years has been to emphasise their pragmatism – that by accepting the ways of the Washington consensus to a greater or lesser extent, economies would grow and everyone would benefit. As such, the state was largely an instrumental institution. What we need now are ethical states – ones that express and explain that the steps their populations must take are moral as well as practical. If states do not have ethical agendas – for example, if they declare that the welfare of future generations should only be a secondary concern of societies today, as is implicit in the stance of free market capitalism through its promotion of consumption – then they will lack the necessary authority to realize change now.

In recent decades, governments across Asia have largely foresworn their ethical responsibilities. In adopting growth as their goal and reducing government intervention and regulation to give markets a greater say, they effectively surrendered much of their claim to any moral legitimacy. Instead, their claim to rule has been based on instrumental grounds: that they could deliver prosperity.

To reclaim a wider legitimacy they must give a much greater priority to their responsibility for taking care of the well-being of those alive now and future generations. They must establish the rules that contribute to this, but of equal importance – maybe even more so if they are to gain the popular support that will make this task easier – they must be able to claim that what they are doing is ethically and morally correct.

States that can be strong and interventionist can protect the resources people will need for development, yet also allow individual and collective freedoms to flourish. Due to variations in culture, society and levels of wealth, we can expect sizeable differences between these states. Some countries will be more rule driven, others more consensus oriented. Some will make relatively fast progress in making themselves more centred around resource management; others may lag badly. Some will be democratic, while others may opt for continued strong rule by a single party.

What they will have in common is a recognition that development can only be equitable if it guarantees an environment with resources in which future generations can also exist. With this priority at the centre of their policy making, they will emerge looking very different from Western liberal democracies. This should not be seen as either a failing or an improvement, but rather as necessary to tackle the predicament in which they find themselves: being presented with the option of consumption-driven capitalism but having to refuse it.

Meat production
Million tonnes

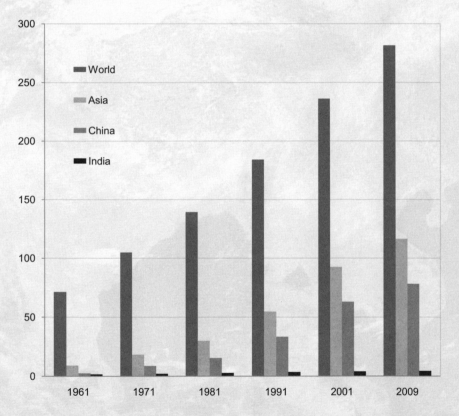

Source: Food and Agriculture Organisation of the United Nations

5

REWRITING THE RULES

The rules of capitalism were written in the countries of the West. From trade and tax practices to corporate governance and accounting standards, almost every business practice has had its regulations shaped by the needs of America and Europe. In the last few years there has been a clamour from many developing countries for change – in the current round of World Trade Organization negotiations, over rich countries' farming and agricultural policies, and at Copenhagen over global warming. Progress has been slow or non-existent.

But, as the last chapter suggested, countries across Asia should not wait for global consensus before acting on environmental issues. They should press ahead now and rewrite the rules governing how their societies and economies use resources and ecological services. Chapter 3 outlined three tenets that Asian governments must use to rethink their future – that resources are constrained, that use must be shared equitably between current and future generations and that re-pricing them would be the key to producing change, leading to sustainable societies and economies.

This chapter returns to these tenets in more detail, constructing a framework in which they can be examined and which, in turn, can be used to generate specific policies tailored to the needs of individual countries. The result is a new way of looking at government policy making that puts the management of resources, including their impact, at the centre.

The overarching goal is the creation of a system robust enough to resist the pressures of political elites, corporate interests and self-serving individuals, yet straightforward enough that it can be realistically implemented and enforced by existing bureaucracies. At its heart, it is a solution that relies on giving the vast majority of people and companies incentives to use fewer resources and produce fewer emissions and pollutants, but which will create the conditions for them to benefit in the short run, and for future generations to benefit in the longer term.

The outcome will be a profound change, one that results in societies moving in the direction of ecological sustainability and social equity, giving them ways of redirecting the energies of individuals and businesses. It will also lead to societies that are more egalitarian and better positioned to lift the poor out of poverty than the ones we have now. Finally, it will also achieve its results without coercion, though it will require the support of states strong and bold enough to oversee the implementation and enforcement of the policies they devise.

Resource-centred policy-making

A society's long-term well-being is determined by two things. The first is its productive base – the resources it has, including its natural resources, its people and its economic institutions (farms, companies, banks, and so on). The second is how it puts these to use.

Since the industrial revolution, enormous attention has been paid to both aspects. The productive base has grown, sucking in ever more resources, requiring ever more people with ever more skills and knowledge. Economic institutions have multiplied in number, size and variety. Much attention has been paid to producing the social and cultural environment that supports this growth, from the introduction of universal education to the establishment of legal systems supported by the necessary enforcement agents. Today, however:

...the depletion of environmental assets is not counted properly in economic calculations, and consequently investment projects that are judged to be commercially profitable are not infrequently socially unprofitable. They are unprofitable because they are rapacious in their use of natural

resources, and they are rapacious because the resources are underpriced. Such underpricing not only affects investment decisions but also may bias the direction of technological change against the natural environment.[1]

Tackling this underpricing of environmental assets lies at the heart of creating sustainable societies. Only by including the cost of using resources or ecological services, of creating pollution or releasing emissions that will have to be treated in the future, can countries reverse the degradation they are now subjecting their land, water, air and populations to.

Some resources have already been depleted to the point where they can only be saved through outright bans on their exploitation. Many fisheries and forests fall into this category. Others, such as water in some parts of the world, need to be subjected to curbs and quotas. But many more , ranging from coal and iron ore to fresh air and soil, exist in abundance (though we should not be fooled by those who point to abundance in some areas as an excuse for relentless exploitation). The issue with these is not a lack, but the need to control the manner and impact of their use. For this last category countries must devise mechanisms that take into account environmental externalities largely ignored until now, focusing the attention of their development strategies on the preservation of their country's productive base over time rather than its exploitation in the short term.

Priority areas

When we look at where we must effect change that reduces resource consumption sharply, three areas stand out. The first is reorienting consumption patterns at all levels of society, including companies, individuals and government. Second is ensuring that the basic needs of all are met, particularly for food, water, shelter and gainful work. And third is shaping the physical environment in which human activity takes place.

Corresponding to these three areas are three core targets for government intervention:

1. Fiscal measures – tax and other financial incentives aimed at reducing resource usage and emissions, encouraging recycling and reuse and

encouraging value-adding labour.

2. Land-management practices – land use measures that prioritize ecological food production and water conservation.

3. Social resource practices – developing rural and urban environments that are both sustainable and allow people to flourish.

These three sets of measures overlap, and should mutually reinforce each other. Nonetheless, each has its own clearly distinct set of goals and techniques, as a closer examination of each one reveals.

Fiscal measures

Constraints on the use of resources will be the core element in any policy programme aimed at producing sustainable economies. For this, it is imperative that the current underpricing of resources and emissions is reversed. This calls for stiff taxes on greenhouse gas emissions and all uses of natural resources. Specific societies would have to figure out exactly what they were charging and how to implement their own systems, but it would be crucial that these taxes be applied across the board – from agriculture and mining to manufacturing and, where appropriate, service industries.

Broad-based carbon taxes are the obvious first step. Such measures alone would strongly encourage companies and individuals to use fewer resources and use them more efficiently. They would have a broad impact on transport costs, discouraging the production of goods using components flown in from around the world, and encouraging manufacturing closer to its intended user, using locally available inputs.

Moreover, countries would all be relatively free to decide the appropriate rates for their own specific conditions. Adjustments for differences in rates between different countries could be made when goods cross borders, with countries with high resource and emission charges imposing duties on products from less rigorous locations, and vice versa.

But discouraging the use of resources would only be half the story. Simultaneously, countries across Asia must encourage the use of their greatest single resource – their people. Obviously, the simple measure of making the inputs of material and energy used in manufacturing more expensive through resource and emission charges would encourage a move in this direction. But it can be driven in other ways, especially by lowering taxes, particularly on income or other labour charges.

Former US vice president Al Gore has advocated such measures – as have American conservatives – proposing that all payroll taxes be eliminated and replaced with pollution taxes aimed at collecting the same amount of revenue.[2]

Such changes in taxation levels would be made in part to compensate individuals for the greater cost of a wide range of goods subjected to resource and emission charges. But its more important goal would be to shift the balance of incentives away from the emphasis on labour productivity that has dominated capitalism through its history, replacing it with an emphasis on using labour to enhance value.[3] These changes would encourage companies to use more people and fewer resources, so encouraging manufacturing economies to become far more service-oriented ones – a goal many countries are already pursuing, given that service industries usually bring higher returns than industrial ones. For the manufacturing that continued, these measures would encourage both companies and individuals to concentrate on developing skills that allow them to add value to the materials they work with.

Walter Stahel, a Swiss architect whose work centres on sustainable manufacturing systems, has explored these ideas in his book *The Performance Economy*.[4] An important part of this would be 'dematerializing' production – making things with far less or even no material. One example of this is digital products – books or music. Another would be the use of 'coldzymes' in detergents, allowing clothes to be washed in cold instead of hot water. And, of course, there are the many electronic devices whose capacity has increased many times as their size has shrunk, such as computer hard drives and memory storage.

Stahel singles out India, China and Japan as countries with the biggest potential to implement his ideas. Japan, because it is already focused on becoming a hydrogen society; China and India because they face resource shortages, and have far less capital committed and less locked-in technology than developed Western countries.[5]

Companies can be encouraged to use far fewer resources in their products through legislation that mandates limits for emissions, energy efficiency and wastage. They would then have a real incentive to find ways of getting more value from every kilo of material they used instead of trying to process as much material as possible – as is now the case with much manufacturing.

Companies that focus on selling the service provided by the product they make rather than the product itself will find themselves incentivized to make multifunctional goods that can be used and reused. Examples here are goods that are leased rather than sold. Naturally, the owner of such goods would want them to be long-lasting, but they might also find themselves selling 'systems' instead of products – as we are seeing with the emergence of cloud computing in place of traditional computer software.

To help move towards these kinds of usage, Stahel advocates using measures that emphasize wealth rather than flow, such as measuring education and health levels rather than the expenditures used by the traditional measures of gross domestic or national product (GDP and GNP). Other measures that can encourage an emphasis on labour-intensive work are forms of taxation that encourage job sharing or working fewer hours (an approach that has worked in parts of Europe, notably France). More radical notions include introducing a basic wage payable to all, reversing the trend towards lowering tax on high earners, and taxing capital and other windfall gains highly,[6] all of which could encourage societies to distribute wealth more equitably while discouraging resource-intensive consumption.

Companies would be discouraged from looking at ways of shortening the product cycle in meaningless ways simply to get more sales – a practice Stahel describes as 'fashion often disguised as a technological progress'.[7]

In Asia, where so many people fall below even the lowest income tax bands, the impact would be less to redirect consumption and more to direct it as people became more prosperous. For the vast majority of people in many of the region's countries, resource and emission taxes, therefore, could be the factor determining consumption patterns before they are established – provided they are introduced rapidly enough.

Taxes can also be used to motivate consumers to recycle and reuse goods, and so extend product lifetimes. Japan and Germany are the world's two most advanced countries as far as recycling is concerned but China, too, is already searching for ways of lowering its use of resources. In 2008, it adopted a 'Circular Economy Law' aimed at encouraging recycling and the reuse of goods and materials. Though vaguely worded,[8] it is clearly part of the measures aimed at lowering its resource usage per unit of economic output. China already accepts that such measures will be necessary if it is to achieve its goal of being a society where every one of its forecast 1.8 billion people is 'moderately prosperous' by 2050. Its State Environmental Protection Administration estimates that, with a per capita GDP four times the current figure, the country will need a sevenfold increase in resource-use efficiency; other Chinese researchers have suggested an even higher figure – around tenfold.[9]

Land-management practices

While industry has been the main driver of resource depletion and environmental degradation, one of the biggest challenges humans face in the next few decades is ensuring everyone has access to safe and affordable food. This will be especially true in Asia. With total demand for food and animal feed expected to double in the region by 2050, the pressure on land for food and the water needed to grow it will be more intense than anywhere else in the world.[10]

At the top of the agenda are investments to protect soil, water resources and biodiversity, and their continued protection through the establishment of land-use practices that have the least ecological impact. As well as having strict management on the use of chemicals and water, this calls for greater local production and labour-intensive techniques, both of which should be encouraged by the principles listed in the previous section.

The industrialization of agriculture needs to be reversed. Agriculture must move towards a regime of low chemical fertilizer, herbicide and pesticide use, replaced where possible by value-adding, labour-intensive techniques. Given that many of the practices of large-scale agro-industry are founded on an underpricing of inputs, the introduction of resource taxes for the raw materials used in agriculture – especially water, but also chemicals – plus emissions tax on the energy it requires and a proper pricing of the impact of run-offs and other pollutants, would inevitably raise costs significantly. Doing so, however, would also encourage a greater use of labour to add value in its place, and so reduce the environmental impact as extensive use of fertilizers and pesticides is curbed.

Governments must introduce policies that encourage the better use of land and protect existing forests, wetlands and wilderness. In the development of plantations, it is vital that companies no longer take two bites at the cherry by securing concessions allowing them first to clear forests and sell the timber, and then gain a second income stream by planting cash crops such as palm trees. Instead, incentives should be devised to encourage the use of the vast tracts of former forest that have been left abandoned once their trees have been felled, particularly in Indonesia and Malaysia.

In many countries, consumption-driven economic growth has already created vast departures from traditional values of moderation. The growing availability of meat is of particular concern because of its inherent inefficiencies as a food source, largely because of the amount of grain that has to be grown to produce feed for livestock.

Water will be the biggest resource issue that much of Asia will have to confront in the next half century. Ten years ago, about 500 million people lived in countries with severe water shortages; by mid century, there will be four billion – most of them in Asia.[11] Pakistan's collapsing water resources were noted in Chapter 1, but at least eight other countries in the region, including India and China, are now officially 'water stressed' by the UN definition of having less than 1700 cubic metres available per person per year. By 2030, supply will only meet 60 percent of demand, according to the Asian Development Bank.[12]

The biggest users of water, by far, are farmers. In India, agriculture accounts for nearly 90 percent of all water used; in China it is 70 percent.[13]

But with most countries in Asia subsidizing or giving away water, much is wasted. Realistic pricing will be a key element of change. Inevitably, raising water prices will result in more expensive food. Overcoming resistance to this will be one of the hardest tasks governments face. Without reform, however, developing countries in Asia face the prospect of having to import up to a quarter of the rice, wheat and corn they will need by 2050.

With harvests in many locations also increasingly affected by drought and heat waves, even in areas where supply was previously plentiful, people are facing rising prices. The growth of international trade in grains and other commodities, accompanied by speculation and hoarding by commodity traders, has exacerbated matters. A key factor in ensuring food supplies and security, therefore, will be raising the status of farming to make it an equal partner in national economies alongside industry and services.

Overall, rural development needs to be given a far higher priority in strategic policy making. Few countries have linked public-sector spending to the protection of these vital resources. If anything, conservation initiatives have been seen as impediments to development – as the cost countries must bear in order to develop, rather than the other way around. The fiscal measures outlined above will help in this. Increasing resource and emission costs will have a big impact on industrialized agricultural practices, making chemical fertilizers and other energy-intensive inputs more expensive. This, in turn, should benefit small-scale local farming of the kind that remains widespread throughout the region.

Asian governments will have to rechannel resources to agricultural and related policy issues so as to rid the sector of the 'poor relation' tag it has endured over the last thirty to forty years. Part of making agriculture central to economic development entails integrating the rural, non-formal sector with reforms in the industrial, manufacturing and services sectors. There has to be a dramatic shift towards this parallel integration so that agriculture is not seen as separate to everything else, but as central to economic vitality and independence.

The rural sector should be treated as a business partner rather than the poor relation of the urban economy. Success in this area, resulting in the creation of more and better jobs in rural areas, would lower the pressure of rural to urban migration in many countries. Integration could usefully focus on improvements to existing inefficiencies in the supply chain which result in food wastages. Estimates suggest that around 30 to 40 percent of fresh produce is wasted in markets like India due to inadequate infrastructure such as transport and storage systems. Reforms of land-ownership rights, access to loans for farmers and availability of insurance can all play a role in transforming rural economies.

With climate change affecting weather and with it harvests, food prices will almost inevitably rise in the coming years. As this happens, governments and consumers may need to overcome long-standing resistance to genetically engineered crops and other biotechnology products. Japanese and South Korean makers of corn starch and corn sweeteners are already using biotech corn; China has experimented with genetically modified rice. Such products should not be seen as panaceas, but they are likely to become an important strand in overall food security strategies. However, they must be subject to strict controls, not just for safety but to ensure that reserves of traditional crops are maintained and countries do not become beholden to multinational agri-businesses, able to force their products on unwilling markets.

Bio-fuels are another product that needs close monitoring. Asian governments must put in place policies to ensure that food prices and production are not affected by fuel production. Certification schemes for bio-fuel products that meet certain stringent criteria with regard to protecting food supplies and ecosystems could play a vital role in this respect.

Finally, fishing stands out as an area badly in need of far stronger regulation. Some three-quarters of the world's ocean fisheries are already either fished out or being fished at or beyond capacity.[14] Asian countries are increasingly responsible for a large part of this over-consumption, particularly in east Asia. Japan, which accounts for a tenth of global fish consumption, now imports 40 percent of what it consumes.

Countries are starting to address the problem. China has summer moratoriums for the Bohai Bay off its north-east coast and in the East China, Yellow and South China seas. Over the last decade it has gradually shrunk both the size of its fishing fleet and total catch targets. Indonesia has imposed various bans and moratoria, including outlawing trawling in its waters as long ago as 1980. But, as with other countries with long coastlines and many islands, overfishing and blast fishing – fishing using explosives – has left the majority of its fisheries depleted.

Governments should explore further the possibility of quotas and regional agreements on no-fish zones, especially in the productive waters of south-east Asia. As has been demonstrated in Africa with measures to protect elephants, rhinoceroses and other animals, the technological and human means already exist to ensure that poaching can be severely restricted if the political will exists.

Broader policies should also include expanding aquaculture, currently dominated by China which produces nearly two-thirds of the world's farmed fish, and stepping up pressure at international forums. The European Union in particular needs singling out for criticism for its continued inability to force various of its members, especially Spain, to stop depleting Mediterranean and Atlantic fisheries to meet Asian demand.

Social resource practices

The third field where governments must rework the rules is in the development of sustainable urban and rural environments where people can flourish. With demand for everything from food, water and energy, to housing, transport and health care all forecast to double or treble by 2050, this will be a major challenge in urban, urbanizing and rural Asia. Some of the broader parameters will be set by fiscal measures that tax resource usage and encourage the land use and related practices already described. But governments will also have to develop social management systems that take responsibility for planning urban and rural settings on a scale that the world has never seen before, with a particular emphasis on transport, energy and education.

In the transport sector, the emphasis must be on providing people with mobility rather than the right to own and use private cars. Emissions and resource taxes will go a long way by themselves to internalize the environmental costs of motor vehicles, but other external factors – including congestion, accidents, noise, and the impact of road building on land-use and landscapes – must also be included in the price of driving. At the very least, charges on vehicles should incorporate their weight, the distance they travel, their emissions and the congestion they cause.

Currently, the approach is the opposite – to subsidize car use by building roads. This encourages more people to drive, which in turn leads to government spending on increasing capacity, which only leads to more traffic. But the consequences of continuing to exclude external costs are that public transport remains disadvantaged: it receives no benefits from sharing its environmental impact among far more users. The failure to incentivize the use of public transport leads to higher traffic volumes. Cars have a huge impact on how land is used; providing for cars is the most important factor in urban and regional planning.

This must be reversed. While Asia will continue to have urban centres – almost certainly growing ones – it should not accept ever-increasing urbanization as its ultimate social goal. With such a high number of people still living in rural areas, governments, particularly in China and India, should start exploring the possibilities of dispersed development built around networks of smaller towns and villages with strong locally oriented economies.

Within and between such communities transport systems will be necessary that provide more than first-class public transport – looking at ways of increasing individual mobility while using the fewest resources. There are already many ideas available; what is needed are far more tests and experiments to see what can be made to work in different types of places.

Falling technology prices could help this search for new transport options enormously. Transaction costs for toll collection, for example, have reached a point where they are no longer a hindrance to introducing electronic road pricing systems. Political will remains the biggest obstacle. Singapore introduced the world's first urban road congestion pricing scheme in 1975, upgrading it to an electronic road system in 1998. The Hong Kong government, despite first discussing an electronic scheme in the 1980s, has never overcome the opposition of transport interests, opting instead to build more roads.

Future systems could go far beyond road pricing. By integrating communications, location and internet technologies, for example, travellers for short as well as long journeys could arrange their travel by booking into networks of local taxis and buses, train or light rail networks, even bicycle hires, that allow them to make journeys as quickly – maybe even more quickly – than they could with private cars. Certainly it is not utopian to suggest that there must be alternatives to the gridlock that many cities experience, in both the West and Asia.

Suggestions that preventing people from driving their cars would be an insufferable attack on their rights should be met by pointing out that few people actually have this 'right' in Asia. Outside Japan and a handful of cities, car ownership remains a minority practice across the region. A key policy imperative for establishing sustainable societies would be to keep them that way. Where cars are permitted, their resource and environmental costs must be included in the price of purchase and operation.

This in turn points to the wider point that in all fields of social resources, societies must ensure that individual rights are not allowed to outweigh collective ones. In transport, it is vital to escape the grip of the automotive industry and its interest in having privately owned cars as people's principal means of mobility. For education, expenditure must be directed at raising the standards of schools across the board, not just at allowing the production of an elite. And in the use of energy, no one must be allowed to believe that their wealth or status allows them to avoid the constraints that everyone else must face. In the Asia of the future, the private jet should have no place.

National energy systems must be extensively reworked by the introduction of serious emission and resource charges. At a stroke, coal and other fossil fuels would lose the price benefits that allow them to dominate many country's power industries. But these must also be supplemented by other government-mandated measures, including aggressive energy efficiency targets for industry, as Japan and South Korea have already done, and as China is starting to do.

Given a rebalancing of costs between energy sources, the widespread uptake of nuclear energy looks increasingly likely to lie at the heart of most national energy policies. Japan, with more than fifty nuclear plants in operation, obtains 35 percent of its electricity from nuclear power. It is the world's third largest nuclear power producer, behind the United States and France. China, however, has the most ambitious expansion programme. Although it only had twelve plants operating as of mid-2008, it has double that number under construction, and has announced plans for total nuclear capacity to be more than forty times its current 9 gigawatt capacity by 2050. India's plans are not so big – it currently has less than half China's capacity, though it foresees more than tenfold growth by 2020.

Education would have to be a priority for all governments. 'Dematerializing' economies will require both knowledge workers and craftspeople, and both in increasing numbers. But schools and universities should have wider goals than simply improving the work prospects of their populations.

Chapter 3 discussed the role of risk minimization as a key tool in tackling the challenges lying ahead; education could contribute to this, producing people who not only have the skills they need to work in the changing world that lies ahead of us, but also have the skills for what Vaclav Smil calls 'the exercise of rational attitudes ... to consider events within longer historical perspectives and trying to avoid the chronic affliction of modern opinion makers who tend to favour extreme positions'. He continues: 'Unrealistic optimism and vastly exaggerated expectations contrast with portrayals of irretrievable doom and indefensibly defeatist prospects.'[15]

People need to change; in Asia, they need to make sure that change takes their societies in sustainable directions. This requires responsible development, which can only be realized by responsible and educated citizens.

Energy, transport, education and other necessary programmes will all require substantial investment, much of it on timescales and with returns that would not appeal to the private sector as it now is, so the state will have to be heavily involved in this spending. That, however, might change. With a very different set of incentives and disincentives in place, long-term investments in social goods may look a lot more attractive than they are now, especially given that growth would take on a rather different meaning in societies looking to increase what individuals could earn through adding value via their time rather than processing large volumes of materials. Education focused on the ethics of consumption would also help.

Resource-centred societies

By putting resource constraints at the centre of policy-making, societies will rework the price framework in which people and enterprises organize and structure their operations. More areas will be off-limits, and those that remain on-limits will be subjected to mechanisms that include environmental costs which until now have largely been ignored. In all this, the big change will lie in putting values on things humans have long taken for free or nearly free – the environment in which we live and the resources it provides us with. Doing so will change the relative incentives and disincentives between different types of activities, depending on their need for resources and demand on ecological services.

As the rules under which people live their lives change, so will their preferences. We will find societies with fewer global goods and greater local choice, less long-distance travel but far superior local mobility, perhaps to the point of allowing us to redefine what 'local' means.

Incentives to use fewer materials will result in goods that last longer, are recycled or reused more. Far more food will be produced much closer to where it is eaten. Crops will be grown with far fewer chemical inputs and maybe using more labour-intensive techniques. Water-intensive crops would be disadvantaged, as would most meats, especially beef, but the majority of foodstuffs would have low energy and other resource inputs. Local produce would require less transport and wastage would be sharply reduced. Labour-intensive farming could also result in increased variety and higher quality, allowing people to have better, tastier and healthier diets.

Would life be more expensive? Relative prices of goods and services will certainly change, with some becoming far more expensive and others far cheaper in comparison. Simply declaring that people will have to pay more overall, however, would be seriously misleading. In the longer term – over the space of several decades, and probably far sooner – average living standards will rise across the board. Even with the most stringent constraints on consumption, companies would continue to look for new sources of value and profit.

It is not only spending and consumption patterns that would change, but also lifestyles and outlooks. Aside from seeing a sharp drop in resource-intensive consumption, it would seem plausible that people would spend more on services and maybe more on shared or community-oriented purchases. Lifestyles, likewise, would be similarly reworked – with more time spent on non-material-related activities, less on anything that required resource inputs: golf and car racing might be out, but badminton and social dancing more popular. Less time spent working might be another consequence.

But predictions – like prescriptions – would be a mistake. The world we now have, with its distinctive economic structures and consumption patterns, was created by a set of incentives that encouraged the utilization of woefully underpriced environmental resources and services. Sustainable societies accept that resources vital for life now and in the future cannot be run down. They have to redirect human ingenuity towards discovering new sources of affluence from different combinations of resource inputs, ones that emit far less pollution and greenhouse gases.

Capitalism can play a vital role in this. As Jeffrey Sachs has noted: 'Modern businesses, especially the vast multinational companies, are repositories of the most advanced technologies on the planet and the most sophisticated management methods for large-scale delivery of goods and services. There are no solutions to the problems of poverty, population and environment without the active engagement of the private sector, and especially the large multinational companies.'[16]

With markets continuing to set prices according to the dictates of supply and demand but within a framework that includes the cost of their environmental factors, we would still expect 'efficient' outcomes, in the economists' definition of the term. Marketing aimed at encouraging consumption would be controlled. Public campaigns aimed at constraining consumption would be widespread. And business strategies would be different because of this. Companies would find ways of extracting value from longer-lived goods, from services built around the performance of their goods rather than their sale, and from reselling and recycling their materials and components.

Technology will have a crucial role, even more so than today. 'Weightless' products – such as digitally delivered words, sounds and images – would be highly favoured. So would information systems aimed at managing materials that were used in the most cost-effective manner. Technology could play a major role in the encouragement of dispersed development by weakening the links between wealth and major metropolitan centres, and so lessening the relentless pressure to create mega-cities.

But even more important than technology, changed incentives, increased mobility and more efficient energy systems will be changes in values. To a degree, these changes will be forced. Asia has no choice but to look for alternatives. Across Asia, people can still expect to harness the forces that have driven the various improvements in standards of living of the last few decades – including economic liberalization, overseas investment and technologies that have helped transform people's lives for the better. They can even expect that, as development occurs, individuals will be able to choose what to consume from a growing array of offerings. What they will not be able to expect, however, is for the individual consumer to be placed centre stage. In Asia, the formula for high standards of living must be different: no one, not even the richest, can expect to consume in a way that endangers the well-being of others, whether they are alive now or will be in the future.

As this chapter has shown, the key to resolving this challenge in Asia is putting resource management at the centre of policy making. Doing so will have a profound effect on lives. It will shape what and how individuals consume, the directions in which companies take their businesses, how food is produced and how water is used and how the balance of urban and rural living is reworked. It will require governments to take a leading role in setting and enforcing new rules, particularly in pricing environmental factors into all aspects of economic and social life (and where necessary going beyond this – to outright bans on the exploitation of a range of natural assets, such as depleted fisheries, forests, minerals and other materials).

If societies across Asia were to incorporate the new rules described in this chapter, not only would they transform themselves domestically, but their interests would also change internationally. As they developed, due both to the scale of Asia's economy overall and the size of its biggest nations, it would increasingly find itself in position to start exercising influence on the nature of change in the rest of the world – an influence with the potential to be enormously positive, as the next chapter explores.

Energy use
Kilogrammes of oil equivalent per capita

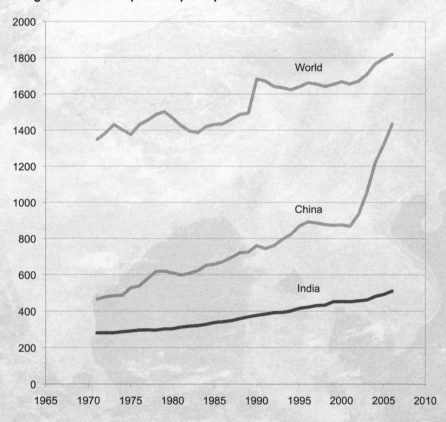

Source: World Bank

6

ASIA AND THE WORLD

The countries of Asia must stop waiting for the West to lead and instead find the confidence to go their own way. For too long they have allowed their futures to be defined in developed-world terms – as 'emerging markets' or 'investment destinations', as 'export-oriented' or as a 'pent-up' source of enormous consumer demand. Now they must identify and pursue their own long-term sustainable development strategies. And they should do this regardless of what is happening in the rest of the world.

The principal objection to unilateral action is that countries should be taking action together. If they do not, then there is little purpose in any one country – however big – making changes, as whatever progress it makes will be rendered meaningless by the lack of change in other countries. Thus, even if the countries of Asia were to transform themselves into genuinely sustainable societies, so long as the West continues with its consumption-driven way of life their achievements would be of little purpose; the world would continue to move inexorably towards further and greater environmental crises. Moreover, acting unilaterally could heighten the risk of clashes, both between Asia and the West and within the region. Surely we should be looking for greater international cooperation, not less?

These points have some substance. There is little hope of achieving a sustainable world if the rich countries continue to base their economic growth on ever-expanding consumption, helped in the United States' case by debt and a fast-growing population. (Its population is forecast to increase by a third, suggesting another enormous leap in its resource usage.) Moreover, if a major Asian country – China, say, or India – were unilaterally to impose stiff carbon and resource taxes on imports, it could find itself embroiled in trade clashes with Europe and America that would undermine cooperation on other issues.

But such fears are overblown. The coming years will be difficult ones for all countries. Climate change will hurt people on every continent. The emergence of China and India will unsettle global power balances. Resource shortages will push up commodity prices and cause food and other crises.

International negotiations on the world's most pressing issues – climate change at the UN and food at the World Trade Organization – have little prospect of progress. Countries, therefore, will have little option other than to act unilaterally. By doing so earlier rather than later, they will find themselves better positioned to protect and strengthen themselves – which could ultimately leave them in a better position to reach genuinely meaningful international agreements a little further down the road.

Get real

Realism must lie at the heart of Asian action. Speaking at the Copenhagen climate change conference in 2009, Brazil's president, Luiz Inácio Lula da Silva, called on the rich countries to take responsibility for their past: 'We need to take measure of each nation's historic emissions so that each of us pays according to its own responsibility.' As the source of most the world's greenhouse gas emissions, the developed nations should bear most of the cost of halting and reversing climate change, installing clean energy technology in poorer countries along the way.

It is a familiar call, often echoed by China, India and other developing countries. And it is one that is just as routinely dismissed or ignored by the West. So why is it made? Essentially for posturing reasons. No leader of a developing country expects anything to change as a result, but such calls play well at home.

But they are also a little disturbing. By demanding that the rich countries take responsibility, they betray a continuing tendency to look to the West for answers – something the West is all too happy to go along with.

Progress on policy to combat climate change must be conducted at the national level of developed countries first of all, says Anthony Giddens, a university professor and close adviser to the UK prime minister Tony Blair: 'The industrial countries must take the lead. We know that the developing countries will not do a lot unless they have a clear-cut example to follow.'[1]

Yet, for the West to continue to see the world's future as resting in its hands is hubris at its worst. The rich world has an appalling record of action in countering the environmental degradation it has wrought around the world. In the first decade of the twenty-first century, the world's rich countries have continued to increase their total emissions of carbon dioxide both in total and on a per capita basis – with the cuts achieved by a handful of European countries more than offset by growth in other nations. If the offshoring of carbon-intensive goods to manufacturing locations in Asia and other parts of the world is included, their record is even worse.[2]

Other moral arguments that the West should change its ways are also likely to fall on deaf ears. Does anyone really think that the developed countries will forgo economic growth in order to leave room for the poorer countries to expand their economies? Or that the populations of America and Europe will start concluding that they have reached a point of prosperity beyond which further expansion will bring no additional happiness?

There are plenty of people advocating these and other similar measures. But, of course, no one is listening. Instead the rich countries are continuing to drag their feet and look for other culprits to blame.

Despite their wealth, there is strong resistance by the rich countries to make a major commitment to mitigation because of a perception that the developing world would be given a free ride. In the aftermath of the Copenhagen conference, China was widely held responsible for the meeting's failure to reach a binding agreement. Since then it has been more and more widely blamed as being the main obstacle to change, with additional charges including responsibility for forest destruction across south-east Asia and resource exploitation in Africa.

There is irony in this. Resistance to change is more deeply rooted in the West than in Asia. A sharp fuel tax rise in China might result in protests, but at least it is possible to envisage the government taking such a step. Bringing US petrol taxes into line with those of Europe is politically unthinkable.[3] Moreover, researchers have discovered that the rich-world democracies are in general more likely to reach and sign international environmental agreements than developing countries. But, as the Kyoto agreement has shown, they are also unlikely to meet the commitments they have made. Promises to deliver technology and aid made in the UN Framework Convention on Climate Change signed in 1992 have still not been fulfilled.[4]

Western failure

Why this failure by the rich countries to act? To focus on a lack of responsibility is too simplistic. Rather, we need to examine the underlying interests at stake – the protection of wealth and power.

Of greatest importance is the reality that as climate change really starts to affect people's lives in profound ways, the rich countries have a better capacity to adapt and cope than the rest of the world.

Drastic steps towards large-scale climate change mitigation could not be taken without a consensus, or at the very least a substantial majority in favour of such measures. But there are many forces acting against the formation of a such a consensus. Powerful industries, among them the automotive, oil and transport-related sectors, are against change.

Against such a backdrop, calls for responsibility are a waste of time. Nations are responsible for protecting and furthering their own interests. In the rare instances where they have acted to assist other countries, it is almost always because their own interests were at stake. Humanitarian assistance, where it has occurred and not been undertaken purely out of self-interest, has been tiny in scale and driven by individuals or non-governmental bodies.

The environmental and climate threats the world faces today make no difference to this. It may be in the interests of all countries not to see the planet ruined, but in figuring out how to avoid this each country has to consider its own interests, striving to find a way forward that best suits it.

As has already been mentioned in this book, there is no single answer that will fairly share the costs between different countries. Because of varied national interests, there can never be agreement on what an appropriate outcome should be. Some countries can tolerate or adapt to more change than others. Some can afford to pay more. And some have the muscle to make others pay for them. China's view of an acceptable outcome will not be the same as Canada's, and Indonesia's will be different from that of the United States – and that is before differences within countries are taken into account.

Consequently, it is pointless to hope that the world's countries will find a universal notion of responsibility and then act on it. The rich nations will not opt to halt or reverse growth while the poor catch up; the developing world will not forgo growth while the rich countries try to figure out if they can maintain their current lifestyles in a sustainable manner.

No surrender

Given this impasse, should Asian countries throw up their hands and surrender to fate? Of course not. Taking refuge in defensive finger pointing, epitomized by rejecting any effort aimed at reining in their energy consumption as an attempt to derail their development, is not an option either.

For the countries of Asia, the failure of the rich countries to come up with their own strategies for coping with climate change and other environmental threats is reason enough to devise their own programmes. The cynicism in the West's outlook must be accepted as part of the reality shaping the challenge that the rest of the world has to live with. So they should look at how they can determine their own fate, not only because they may be able to improve their own conditions, but because they also have the potential to play a major role in determining the planet's eventual fate – possibly more so than the rich countries.

The primary reason for embracing change is that Asia – as this book has repeatedly stressed – has no future in continuing on its current trajectory. If countries across the region individually try to maximize their own growth rates in order to put them in a better position to attempt to mitigate and adapt to environmental threats in the future, then each will have its position worsened by both its own actions and those of other countries – a classic case of the prisoner's dilemma.

Already the region is at its limits. Of the world's seven biggest emitters of carbon dioxide, four are Asian – China, India and Japan, by dint of their fossil-fuel and other resource-intensive industries, and Indonesia because of its deforestation.[5] Not only will continuing down the consumption-fuelled path lead to environments becoming more degraded and depleted, but countries will expose themselves to an ever greater likelihood of international clashes – over resources, particularly energy and water, and quite possibly over food as well as trade.

In contrast, putting resource management at the centre of their policy making would bring multiple benefits – above all, that countries would start to confront directly the limits that one way or another will eventually constrain their future. And once this initial step has been taken, not only can countries begin to get a handle on the difficulties they will have to overcome in imposing resource restraints, but the range of possibilities they may be able to exploit will also begin to form.

Nowhere could adopting a risk-minimization framework prove more useful than here. Improved land-use systems and urban development aimed at dispersing development and avoiding the construction of mega-cities would go a long way towards helping countries improve their food and energy security – two of the biggest concerns of Asia's most populous countries.

There are no grounds for believing that countries in Asia would suffer great damage by unilaterally introducing stiff prices on resource use and environmental services. Assuming that foreign investment remained desirable, fears that attractiveness to overseas businesses might diminish would not be justified. For sure, some costs would rise, but others – particularly labour, if income taxes and other labour fees were cut – should remain attractive.

With labour cheaper related to material inputs, such measures would promote the development of service industries, as well as craft and other more labour-intensive industries. By encouraging skilled work and innovation aimed at extracting more value from less material, companies would be encouraged to move up the value chain more rapidly than if they were to continue to rely on underpriced resource inputs.

The markets of the region would continue to have the appeal they now exercise, though with the form of consumption they encouraged utterly recast. In China, for example, private consumption would continue to be a motor of development, but only of goods and services that had a low environmental impact. So if it were to introduce a carbon tax levied on all goods sold in the country, both those made domestically and imported, it would be an extremely powerful force in encouraging manufacturers both domestically and outside its borders to lower the carbon content of their products.

By adopting resource-centred policy making, countries would be sending a clear signal of the priorities others should adopt when dealing with them. Governments could finally end the rich world's obsession with market-opening measures. With growth no longer the over-riding priority, calls by developed countries for greater access to the markets of Asia would no longer have the power they have had in recent decades.

Instead, governments would have alternative ways of assessing which services and goods they were prepared to allow entry to, and which they might prefer to refuse. In farming, for example, the greater encouragement and preservation of indigenous practices, especially those which supported local jobs, might result in fewer opportunities for the industrial agriculture that multinational agri-businesses like to impose. More broadly, countries would be able to say 'no' when multinationals and their supporters attempted to force unnecessary or inappropriate forms of consumption on their populations.

Stiff emissions and resource taxes would go a long way towards discouraging developed-world industries from offloading their polluting or resource-intensive industries to Asia. In the future, the companies that would be welcomed would be those which could enhance resource productivity and labour value in the production of better-performing goods, ones that require far fewer material inputs.

Adopting a tough attitude towards resources management could make it easier for countries to reach further deals, like Norway's 2010 agreement with Indonesia to pay $1 billion for a two-year deforestation moratorium.[6] Rich countries would clearly prefer to pay for such agreements if they could be sure they would be adhered to.

No alternative

The alternative to the resource-management route – continuing down a resource-hungry, consumption-driven path – could only exacerbate existing issues. A regional race for resources would only breed more resentment and competition, possibly even spilling over into war.

Within Asia, water resources are particularly problematic. The Himalayas and Tibetan plateau are home to the sources of rivers that provide water to countries embracing nearly half of the world's population. Increasingly used for hydroelectric projects as well as agriculture, upstream utilization of these rivers could devastate the lives of hundreds of millions of people – with one country, China, able to influence matters like no other. As Kenneth Pomeranz has pointed out, not only is it the source of most of the rivers flowing from the Himalayas, but it has the finance and engineering expertise to develop any dam project it sees fit.[7]

Some countries are trying to avert resource shortages by leasing land in other countries. In 2008, Daewoo of South Korea announced an agreement with Madagascar to farm 3.2 million acres on a ninety-nine-year lease, specifically citing 'food security' concerns.[8] In early 2010, Kazakhstan was considering leasing land for farming to China.[9]

But such schemes can easily backfire, worsening ties between countries or exacerbating resource problems. When news of Kazakhstan's plan leaked out, protestors launched anti-Chinese rallies, while Madagascar's continued reliance on World Food Programme aid makes the idea of producing grain for export to an already well-developed country look simply wrong.

The problem with such solutions is that they look to maximize resource supplies rather than minimize resource use. So long as such an approach dominates thinking, then both Asia and the world will only see growing tensions and conflicts as countries seek to control the finite number and size of resources available.

Again, risk minimization is a useful method for circumventing the dilemmas conventional approaches find impossible to escape. In looking to minimize risks, countries would obviously want to search for actions that would lower the likelihood of conflict while realizing positive gains in other areas. Curbing resource use wherever possible would patently fall into such a category.

Whereas the West has reasons for wanting to avoid or delay change in the hope – albeit desperate – that something may turn up, alleviating the need for desperate action, Asia has the opposite issue: a way of controlling the change that is already taking place in order to create societies that are both different from now and different from those existing in the West. Its issues are largely to do with finding something new, not preserving what it has.

By acting boldly and purposefully, countries in Asia can help themselves face the real threats of environmental degradation and resource depletion that they are already encountering, and come up with solutions that will work to their own advantage in the long run.

Introducing emissions and resource taxes at a national level could prove a far better way to reach international environmental agreements than trying to bring countries together and reach agreements first at huge conferences, such as that in Copenhagen.

As proposed in Chapter 5, it would be relatively straightforward for Asia's major economies to implement an emission tax within their own borders. They could then move on to reach bilateral or regional agreements. In all such agreements, precise harmonization would not be necessary. As long as emission levels were broadly in line, adjustments could be made when goods crossed borders.

Over time, countries which had low or no emission charges would find themselves losing out. With their exports taxed when they were imported by overseas buyers, they would have no trade advantage. And over time they would also likely lose in international competitiveness due to the lower level of incentives in their domestic market for curbing resource use.

Changes such as these could have major knock-on effects around the world. They have the potential to be a major force pushing the widespread imposition of broad-based carbon taxes. They could also undermine the arguments for the cap-and-trade schemes that Western finance currently backs. By restricting emissions directly at their source, there would be no need for indirect schemes which tend to reward established companies, in both finance and the energy industry, and have already proved readily open to abuse.

Emission taxes also have the advantage of not requiring international negotiations before their levels are set. Cap-and-trade, by contrast, requires countries to reach complex and often contentious agreements balancing a whole range of variables. The most tricky of these are per person emission allowances, and the difficulty of finding agreements that result neither in less-developed countries having to accept lower per capita allowances than rich countries, nor rich countries paying extra for their energy and then handing large sums to the developing countries they increasingly see as strategic competitors.

But the biggest potential benefit of going down such a route is that Asia could find itself the driving force towards global environmental agreements, particularly for climate change.

A Beijing consensus?

Given the growing power and influence of China both within the region and worldwide, should other countries be looking to China to take the lead?

Within the last decade, there have been major changes in the relative perceptions of its strength. When it was negotiating its entry into the World Trade Organization, both the United States and the European Union were able to secure major market-opening victories. In the decade since, and particularly since the global financial crisis, Chinese confidence has risen strongly. It now vigorously defends its interests in international bodies and has started to take ever more confident international steps, be it extending its commercial and resource interests in other parts of Asia, Africa and Latin America, or at such an event as the Copenhagen climate change conference of 2009.

Various commentators have suggested that we are already seeing signs of what has been labelled a 'Beijing consensus' – loosely defined as a combination of strong government oversight of the economy, large-scale investment in infrastructure, support for manufacturing via tax breaks and other incentives, a compliant labour force, tightly controlled financial markets, and strict management of the exchange rate and capital flows.

The advantages – especially to those looking for an alternative to the West's market-democracy formula – are twofold: first, that the financial excesses that caused the global financial crisis can be avoided, and second, that officials have a greater freedom to act without being subject to the short-term pressures created by having to meet the demands of an electorate.

The shortcoming of Beijing's strong-government approach is the assumption that having its hands less tied makes it easier for a government to make the 'right' decision. In fact, it is quite possible for authoritarian rule to be a hindrance to change. Vested interests often find it easier to retain their positions, as they have fewer people to buy off, are subject to less scrutiny by the public or the media and would be subject to less punishment in the wake of environmental or other disasters. Indeed, there is no intrinsic reason why an authoritarian regime would find it easier to make a 'tough' decision than a democratic one would.

In China's case, the dilemma of choosing between going its own unilateral way or looking for ways of increasing regional and international cooperation is best resolved by considering what would work best for a resource-poor but highly populated nation.

As the United States has found, using its economic muscle to build a powerful military machine does not solve problems. Its energy issues stem from a failure to address how resources are managed domestically. Because of this, energy security remains as much a headache for America as it was when Jimmy Carter tried to address the problem in the late 1970s.

China should learn from this. The possibility of clashes over water flowing from the Himalayas, or oil and gas from fields in the South and East China seas, could lead to an arms race across the region – and far greater tensions with the United States. This would not help solve the resource conundrums it faces. Thus, continuing its economic expansion along a consumption-driven path is likely to result in China's interests colliding with those of other countries.

A far more profitable course would be simultaneously to introduce strong resource constraints within its domestic economy while looking for ways of cooperating with its neighbours in a search to find multilateral responses to cross-border issues, especially for water.

Taking such an approach could lead to a Beijing consensus being replaced by an Asian consensus. Due to the nature of the environmental threats the world faces, no country – even China – will be able to go it alone. But someone has to lead. Countries in Asia have the incentives and the capabilities to be the ones who start, and China has the most pressing interest in initiating such a move.

The best place to do this would be via a regional environment grouping – one focused beyond climate change to look at the environmental challenges the region faces. Such a grouping should take as its starting point the need to put all types of resource management at the heart of policy making – water management; the depletion of renewable resources, notably fisheries and forests; energy and mutual needs for energy security; and the management of trade to take into account the needs of incorporating emissions and resources taxes.

Steps taken so far have been baby ones, such as the Mekong River Commission, set up by Cambodia, Laos, Thailand and Vietnam in 1995, with China and Myanmar joining as dialogue partners a year later. And the fixation remains with pursuing market-opening agreements, such as the range of bilateral free trade and other economic agreements recently signed or under negotiation between countries in Asia. But given the advances the region has made with trade agreements in recent years, notably the China–Asean pact that came into force at the start of 2009, there are strong grounds for believing that cooperation could be extended to environmental and resource issues.

If the countries of Asia can change themselves, they may also find themselves equipped with powerful tools that can help realize change in the rich countries. Top of the list would be the demand for a rewriting of trade rules so that environmental and other negative external costs were included in the prices of goods and services. Throughout this book it has been argued that ecological costs must be included in prices if countries are going to make any form of progress towards establishing sustainable societies. To do this, they simply have to say 'here are the prices that others will have to pay if they want to do business or sell goods in our societies'.

Asian countries could also increase the pressure for changes in international finance, in particular for the introduction of some form of tax on all financial transactions. Finance, having been a great accelerator of change in the last few decades, clearly needs to be constrained to ensure it cannot further the private gain of a few at the expense of the many – especially when it comes to the manipulation of markets in commodities and resources that have a major ecological impact, such as fossil fuels, many minerals and timber. Countries should also note that finance tends not to benefit countries, just financiers. Neither the United States nor the United Kingdom enhanced their long-term sustainability via their overgrown financial sectors.

And they could demand changes in the way in which multilateral bodies such as the International Monetary Fund, World Bank and World

Trade Organization shape policy making in countries around the world. Having been essentially tools of the West, and especially the United States, and so key forces in the spread of market ideology, these organizations need major overhauls if they are to play any sort of role in meeting the environmental needs of the twenty-first century. Where they perhaps have most to contribute is in the coordination of policies – such as how trade and investment could be used to deliver better economic performance with fewer resources rather than simply increasing the overall flow of goods, as is now their overwhelming goal.

None of this would involve Asia looking to have the West over a barrel and demanding change. Rather, by defining the incentives and disincentives that will give their societies inter-generational sustainability, the region's leading economies would be laying the foundations for a new form of multilateralism. This would be one based on mutual agreements over emissions and resource taxation, rather than market access; one which would clearly define which forms of trade should be encouraged and which discouraged, and so would shape development rather than hinder it; and one which would look in the long run to guide all nations towards growth focused on performance rather than throughput, and therefore away from material-based consumption towards increasing the quality and value of labour.

If nothing changes, then there is a high likelihood that the desire of these countries to become major global economies will become a major source of conflict between Asia and the West – with each holding the other responsible for being the main obstacle to tackling the problems of resource depletion, environmental destruction and climate change.

This will lead to tit-for-tat actions across many fronts, including foreign policy, and lead to more polarization and isolationist policies. A taste of what may come was seen at Copenhagen, where the conflicts of interest between developing and developed countries were clearly visible.

But Asia has both the incentives and the abilities to break out of this mould. It can – indeed, should – throw down a challenge to the developed world. To do so, however, it will have to demonstrate that it is changing.

Chapter 5 showed the sort of changes countries in Asia should undertake; the next and final part of the book examines how they can start to do this.

Obviously, there is much speculation in this – but let us say that putting resource management at the centre of policy making could have benefits extending beyond borders. As countries cut their energy and resource needs, they will experience less tension with their neighbours and have greater food and energy security – and because they will be both more secure and have less need for international resources, there will be greater potential for realizing international agreements.

The big mistake would be to think that conventional economic growth would help by putting a country in a stronger position – that is, by strengthening it and so enabling it to have a greater power to get what it wants or to resist pressure from other countries. Going down this route would have entirely the opposite effect. It opens up a country to more risks of conflict – say over resources – and in making it dependent on resources at a time when competition for them will grow more intense, the country will end up becoming weaker.

Male obesity rate
Percentage of male population aged 15-plus

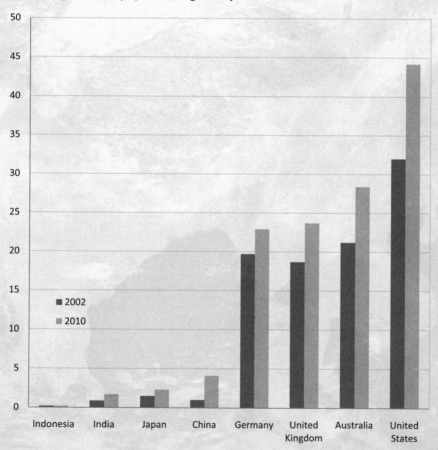

Source: World Health Organisation

CONCLUSION
– RESHAPING CAPITALISM

Asia has the potential to reshape capitalism and create a new economic model for the twenty-first century – one that is genuinely sustainable. To do so it must end capitalism's reliance on underpriced environmental and resource inputs. Countries across the region must rewrite the rules that have driven growth until now. They must reject the consumption-driven ways that powered the West to global dominance and replace them with new practices, ones that constrain human impact on the environment.

Taking this route will upset many. Not just those companies and countries with huge vested interests in today's model of economic growth, but the hundreds of millions, billions perhaps, of people across the region who have been told that they too can aspire to a Western way of life. But if the countries of Asia are to have viable futures of any kind, change must come. Governments, citizens and companies must accept the resource and environmental constraints that confront them.

Action must be taken soon. Asia's current trajectory points towards imminent disaster within a few decades. Noeleen Heyzer, head of the UN's economic and social commission for Asia and the Pacific, suggests just fifteen more years of the current model would be environmentally and socially devastating.[1] Others, including the leaders of most Asian nations, envisage longer time frames. But what cannot be debated is the need to start the process of change now. The old idea must be banished once and for all: it is not possible for Asia to grow first, then clean up afterwards.

We have seen that the conventional solutions of markets, technology and finance – as advocated by so many politicians, business leaders and commentators, particularly those from the rich countries most influential in shaping business thinking – cannot work. This leaves no alternative but a more interventionist state, one aimed at changing social behaviour as well as economic activity. The alternative, however, would be the almost inevitable far greater and far more costly interventions that would be required as climate change and other environmental impacts produced droughts, floods and other disruptions.

We must use the knowledge science has acquired of how to manipulate the power and bounty of nature to work out alternative tools for running our economies – ones that can allow countries to develop, but without destroying the natural assets on which all life is based. To signal its overall intentions, every country should have a chief scientist at cabinet level. Establishing such a post would be an important signal of change, suggesting that whereas before we bowed down to independent central bankers and chief economists, now we should be recognizing the authority of independent scientists.

Realizing change will require the imposition of constraints – via fiscal and other economic tools, and command and control measures. Countries may differ in their approach to resource management, but there is no alternative to imposing strict constraints on the use of material and energy inputs. Emission and resource taxes will be the key tool, along with restrictions on private and public consumption.

Applying these measures will transform national economies. They will lead to new ways of producing food, creating value and determining the landscapes in which people spend their work and leisure time. But their greatest impact will be in the abandonment of the consumption-driven growth model that the world has relied on for the last few decades.

Is change possible?

But is change possible? In particular, can governments find the willpower necessary to embark on projects of transformation that, inevitably, will generate fierce opposition from vested interests?

For some, it would appear self-evident that avoiding catastrophe should be motivation enough for governments to embark on programmes of change. But humans procrastinate; their concerns are about the present, not some hypothetical tomorrow. This is almost certainly an evolutionary trait. But it is one that must be consciously repressed and replaced with a careful consideration of the range of different futures that lie ahead. Unless you believe the most gloomy of forecasters, doomsday is not an immediate prospect. But, depending on the nature of our action or inaction, we face a hugely varying range of environmental breakdowns and catastrophes, some – such as global warming – with a global impact; others – such as pollution from a factory – felt locally.

Moreover, even accepting the need for change tells us nothing about where we should be going instead. While there is widespread agreement that we face some unprecedented challenges and that change is necessary to meet them, what is far from apparent is how to balance the range of interests at stake. Oil and resource companies will want one set of changes; hard-core environmentalists another. Those with little to lose from fast change will advocate 'big bang' approaches; those heavily invested in the current system will argue for a slower pace. With all these conflicting interests and outlooks, how can any government expect to move ahead, let alone form a consensus with other governments on a common programme?

While there are solutions that undoubtedly are wrong, such as trying to build massive mirrors in space to reflect the sun's warmth away from Earth, there is no single set of right answers. What countries will have to do is put forward large packages of policies that simultaneously target a huge range of activities. Each combination of the many options available to us will have benefits and drawbacks. Some of these we will be able to anticipate; many more will be uncertain or unknown. Some options will be appropriate for certain countries, but not for others. Different bundles of options will produce different sets of winners and losers, both within countries and between them. Exactly how they will play out cannot be known in advance. We must accept this uncertainty – and that societies will have to grope their way forward.

There is no utopia out there waiting to be discovered, but for countries looking for a rallying theme, it is the construction of societies that can guarantee a future for the descendents of people alive today. The only route to achieving this is constraint. As the conservationist Caroline Fraser has put it, we must learn to manage 'our appetites, expectations, fears, our fundamental avariciousness. If we do not succeed at that, other forces assuredly will'.[2]

For such a learning process to occur, we need debate. And for debate we need to get the questions we want to pose onto national agendas. If people do not accept the need – indeed the responsibility – for the discussion of these issues, then they can only expect to be subjected to harsher measures in the future. So we must ask what changes need to be made, and how they can be realized. But we must also ask what the benefits of change will be, and who they will accrue to. Who will lose out? Where will resistance come from? Can it be overcome? If so, how? What steps can be taken to push governments in the direction of change – and what changes can governments force their citizens to accept? How important are the differences between countries? Are different political systems better or worse at realizing change? What are the implications of this?

Future vision?

Because of the need for national-level discussions on change, I am reluctant to make country-specific prescriptions. However, there are some principles which can be borne in mind by all governments in considering what lies ahead.

The first is a vision of the future with the power to initiate change and then keep it advancing. Such a vision would need a depth and breadth to convince a broad cross-section of society – from the highest ranks of government to the very poorest – that change would be worth it. It would be one that leaders can believe in and articulate, that policy makers see as feasible, that populations would support and which could overcome the resistance of vested interests.

Articulating such a vision is a tall order. But at its heart must stand the idea of a grander future embracing a wider range of values than the crude appeal to growth that most countries have relied on in recent decades. And it must also have a rather different destination from that implicit in the growth model – of convergence with the rich world. With so much uncertainty over the future, it would be foolish to attempt a detailed portrait, but an outline can be broadly, if roughly, discerned:

- of countries where development flourishes in every corner,

- where people enjoy the advances of technology, but feel linked to both local and national communities,

- where their collective natural and other resources are shared equitably across society and conserved for future generations, and

- where constraints are seen as both a guarantee of sustainability and an incentive to achieve more with less.

Convergence would thus not be targeted at the top, but within societies. Instead of growth, countries should explicitly target a broader public good as the over-riding factor determining the shape of policy decisions. Governments must repeatedly stress that what they are doing is for the benefit of their citizens as a whole. As noted elsewhere, one of capitalism's key claims is that people in general benefit because of the selfish pursuit of their own interests by those who 'innovate' or 'invest' – principally those who already control sizeable assets. But many of these have benefited because they were able to take advantage of resources, particularly ecosystem resources, that they were allowed to exploit cheaply or for free. Governments which put resource management at the centre of policy making would, in contrast, repeatedly point out that natural assets are the property of all and not of the few able to exploit them.

The Indian government is making moves in this direction. It has passed legislation strengthening local rights over community-held land, and at the time of writing it was attempting to pass a mining bill that forces mining companies to share 26 percent of profits with local communities. Of course, companies are often able to ignore such laws, taking advantage of weak bureaucracies and widespread corruption. But the growing ability of environmental officials to confront business, and sometimes overcome it, is a positive sign for the future.

Raising the status of publicly held property would implicitly be more egalitarian than the West's liberal democratic model. By being able to argue that their actions were both environmentally necessary and socially equitable, governments across the region would also do much to advance their claims to legitimacy.

Exactly how the issue of legitimacy is handled will differ from country to country. Those with long traditions of relative equality – Japan, for example – are likely to find it easier than those with greater income disparities between rich and poor. Centralized authoritarian rule has some advantages – China could impose a carbon tax tomorrow. But it also has its weaknesses. Unsubjected to public opinion or market costs, communist regimes outdid all others in creating industries that used more energy to gain worse results than any other system, far outstripping the negative impact of market capitalism.[3]

As was discussed in Chapter 4, however, while democracy may prove beneficial in curbing environmental abuse in rich countries, its institutions are far more easily subverted in poorer countries, especially those where elections are a relatively recent development. More important than the specific form of political system is the quality of its governance. Asia has room for Indian democracy, Chinese-style authoritarian rule and the guided democracy of Malaysia – provided they can deliver policies that enforce constraints on consumption.

Because of the need for good governance, a high priority should be given to institution building and raising the quality of officials. Accountability and transparency will have a role in this, but efficient and effective policy execution must be the primary goal for the immediate future. Given the evidence from a range of countries that a movement towards democracy can undermine good governance, particularly in the short term, developing and maintaining a strong executive capacity is likely to be of crucial importance in realizing the changes countries will have to make in the immediate decades ahead.

Adopting risk minimization as a guiding operational principle should enhance such government. Within a general framework of mitigating the worst excesses of resource depletion and environmental degradation, its realistic approach accepts that there are conflicts between the various goals, and that therefore trade-offs are necessary. In its eschewal of grand solutions, it allows officials to focus on ascertaining and acknowledging how power is distributed in societies now, and then look to bring about change where it is possible, as quickly as possible. Working in tandem, risk minimization and a broader notion of the public good offer governments a foundation from which to launch policies that mix realism with a recognition that support from as broad a cross-section of society as possible is essential, but which retain their ultimate goal of transforming the fundamental operations of society.

Two axes of change

From these principles of an over-riding inter-generational public good, guiding actions shaped within an overall framework of risk minimization, we can now consider the more specific policies governments should be considering.

Up to now, resources and ecological services have been woefully underpriced. By putting a realistic price on our environment through emission taxes and other charges, countries can determine an appropriate direction and rate of development. Pricing them too high would stifle growth, including the growth that we want; pricing them too low would lead to people carrying on abusing them as they now do. But there is no right price. Within a society, different groups have different interests and needs; between countries, these differences can be even greater. This price is essentially political. What must be done is to ensure that those who benefit and those who lose out from this price can be clearly identified – and that shows whether enough is being done to ensure the welfare of both current and future generations by taking into account the cost of resources, emissions and ecological services.

To move forward, governments will have to look at realizing change along two axes. The first is the one explored through this book: constraining the ways in which the environment is used and abused. The second is a reworking of the ideas underlying consumption, emphasising the value of public goods and discouraging positional or status goods. A good example would be replacing domestic flights, especially by private jets, with a high-speed train network. Obviously, a good part of such reworking can be realized through the incentives and disincentives of changing the cost of goods by pricing in environmental factors. But the shaping of attitudes has an equally important role, including creating attitudes in favour of lifestyles with preferences for sustainable consumption.

Social ecology

If we are to move towards sustainable societies in Asia, we must consider how applying the rules for restricting resource usage can be done in the context of everyday life, both when working and relaxing. Chapter 5 outlined a framework of fiscal measures, land-use practices and new approaches to social organization with the potential to create sustainable national economies. Creating sustainable societies, however, would require similar measures to be extended to every area where governments play a role – from social policy and education to culture and even sport.

To do this, we will need to look at the way incentives are structured. What we want are incentives that allow, even encourage, people to consume more – but only in ways that do not increase the demands on our resources, deplete our environment or produce more emissions and pollutants.

An area that could be fruitfully explored is how consumption-driven capitalism has developed techniques to displace traditional outlooks, and whether these can be countered. One example would be the preference for owning over doing: previously children played a game, now they own a PlayStation. Another would be the possibilities offered by traditional cultural attitudes, such as the preference for vegetarian diets in India. We must look for ways in which community values can be strengthened, allowing for a greater number of public goods to be used by all rather than the ownership of 'status' goods by a few. This is particularly relevant for transport. Cities should be built around providing mobility for all, not building more and more roads for private cars.

As Richard Thaler and Cass Sunstein argue in *Nudge*,[4] often the simplest way of securing a positive outcome is to make it the default. In 2009, South Korea introduced rules for home food waste-disposal units that aim to cut domestic food waste by a fifth – users will be charged according to the volume of waste they produce. Restaurants across the country will also have to use standardized kitchenware, aimed at reducing waste by restricting the size of portions.[5]

But once the idea of resource constraints is embraced, governments should not hesitate to apply the logic of their position widely. Hong Kong is the largest importer of live fish in Asia, buying, in particular, from Indonesia and the Philippines. Its imports include endangered fish which are illegally exported from their country of origin; Hong Kong, however, has not made it illegal to buy such imports, so encouraging illegal fishing and smuggling across south-east Asia.[6] Such behaviour is hard to defend now; in the future it should be unthinkable.

Ideas about the way we use and manage resources must be placed at the centre of education. This does not mean brainwashing, but it does allow for aggressively countering the promotion of consumption that lies at the heart of modern advertising. It calls for promoting an awareness of the workings of nature; where energy comes from and how it is used; the life cycles of products and what becomes of them. For too long, schools and universities have been regarded as the training ground for economic growth, be it by preparing people for the disciplines of company life or learning 'marketable' skills. Instead, they should be redirected towards giving people an understanding of the human impact on the world and the consequences that follow from this.

In advertising, governments must ask to what extent companies should be allowed to shape and promote consumption. If the goal is establishing societies that consume within limits, should we restrict the promotion of activities aimed at realizing the exact opposite? Why not introduce a levy on all corporate advertising which is passed to an independent body charged with producing public-interest spots highlighting the impact of consumption?

In many countries, tobacco advertising has been virtually outlawed. Alcohol advertising is also often restricted. And in some countries there are limits on marketing to children – through the banning of billboards near schools, for example. Advertising that encourages consumption needs also to be subjected to constraints, especially when it comes to areas such as promoting goods to children and encouraging resource-intensive activities. So how about a sugar tax? California is considering just such a idea.[7] And if a sugar tax, then why not a fried food tax? Or a meat tax? Countries will have to come up with their own answers to such questions. Singapore famously banned chewing gum because of problems with littering. Other places may have other preferences, perhaps drawn up in response to popular pressure.

In social policy, a key part of putting resource management at the centre of policy making would be stressing just how important the public interest is. This is in stark contrast to the arguments of consumption-driven capitalism, and its claims that allowing everyone to pursue individual self-interest eventually leads to everyone benefiting. This will lead to a strong emphasis on providing the necessities of life and improving the status of the less well-off, and a rejection of the claims that only by allowing the rich to prosper can economic growth be guaranteed.

Alternative wealth

Further into the future, Asian societies must consider whether they are able to create prosperity without resorting to conventional forms of economic growth. Japan is already taking exploratory steps in this direction. Indeed, there is a significant body of opinion which suggests a new look should be taken at the achievements of its supposedly 'lost' decades since the bursting of its economic bubble at the start of the 1990s. Its overall economic growth has been anaemic but, because its population is shrinking, per capita figures have been respectable. And at the same time it has become the world's leader in many areas of sustainability. It is the most energy-efficient of the world's major economies, recycling is a part of daily life and with low income disparities, its social cohesion is not under threat – making it one of the world's safest societies.

But there are ways in which other countries could start moving in such a direction without having to wait for their wealth levels to reach Japanese heights and their populations to go into natural decline. Obviously, stabilizing population size and so putting a cap on resource use should be a major goal of almost every country in Asia. The best way of lowering fertility rates is ensuring people have social and economic security.

Poverty could be tackled directly with programmes specifically aimed at helping the poorest. Trickle-down theories should be rejected because of their assumption that a sizeable segment of society has already gone far beyond meeting their basic needs and so can indirectly support lifting the poorest out of poverty.

Fiscal and labour policies aimed at strengthening local economies could help both to reduce poverty and prevent migration to cities. Much success in both areas could be realized by developing rural credit networks that allowed individuals and small businesses access to funding – not just the micro-credit schemes associated with Bangladesh's Grameen Bank, but at the next level up, which is currently very poorly served by commercial banks. Doing so would encourage the growth of rural social enterprises able to offer both rural jobs and local produce. Curbs on the resource-intensive practices of industrialized agriculture would further aid their development. Where basic living needs are met, employment policies can explore other directions that may reduce consumption, such as shorter working weeks, more support of education and measures that encourage people to regard quality of life issues as extending beyond the amount they earn.

One of the goals of imposing emissions and resource taxes would be to lead a shift towards 'genuine' investment – investment that takes into account the depletion of environmental assets that are now either underpriced or not priced at all. As much of this spending would be undertaken by governments committing themselves more strongly to environmental and ecological assets, we could expect a sizeable shift in investment from private to public goods, especially for longer-term projects with low returns.

Most countries would find themselves running with mixed economies, with state-owned companies active in some sectors (energy and resources), and private ones in others (the majority of service and manufacturing industries). Particularly at a local level, such companies would not need to be big. Across the region, we could expect large-scale investment in long-term schemes to revitalize land and forests, rivers and watersheds, wetlands and fisheries. A key priority here would be creating new enterprises centred on resource management, instead of the resource extraction model now predominant.

Energy networks using renewable sources would be another likely target of state funding. But technologies, particularly government-supported ones, should be aimed at spreading well-being rather than maximizing economic returns; dissemination should perhaps in general be slower than in the past, with an emphasis on forestalling environmental problems rather than treating them.

Many of these actions by themselves would signal that a society's prosperity should be measured in other ways than the rate of its GDP increase – a figure that is particularly problematic in its failure to account for resource depletion and environmental damage. William Bissell, the owner of a $65-million Indian textile business that links 40,000 individual artisans into a nationwide distribution network, suggests measuring poverty by a lack of access to water, food, medicine, education and legal rights, not income.[8] But governments must also back their policies with constant reminders that being well-off involves balancing a range of factors, among them ensuring social equity and an environment fit to be handed on to future generations.

How might societies look?

Given this book's emphasis on constraints, it is legitimate to ask what sort of societies we might see emerging if resource constraints were made the central concern of policy making. In particular, given the billions of people still living in poverty in Asia, would constraints mean people having to remain poor as part of the price of realizing sustainability?

The answer is no. The framework described in Chapter 5 would encourage societies to use fewer resources, and to concentrate on developing work that is more labour-intensive and labour value-adding than the consumption-driven model. Finally, the era where human inventiveness was directed at creating machines aimed at replacing human labour could be over, giving way to a period focused on finding ways of allowing working people to be rewarded for increasing resource productivity.

In such societies, economies will be focused on performance rather than throughput. Efficiency will be defined by how little material and how few resources are used in the manufacture of a product or the delivery of a service, not how quickly it is made or its cost reduced. Productivity will be measured by resource conservation instead of output volume.

The importance of 'patient' work will rise. In agriculture such labour will be the means by which people can improve the productivity of the land while ensuring that food production produces less pollution and conserves soil, water and forests. In other spheres, it will encourage the 'dematerialization' of manufacturing and a far greater share of skilled services, in turn creating a new source of jobs.

Such changes would have some clear impacts in shaping the direction of business. Individuals, companies and governments would all be encouraged to move from manufacturing to services; with steep transport costs for both people and goods, the local would have a strong advantage over the national or international; community businesses would be preferred to remotely owned ones, especially for the management of natural assets, such as forests and watersheds. More industries would be built around the performance of their products, especially ones with enhanced longevity or a higher potential for reuse or recycling. High charges for disposal and waste would promote the development of such goods and the repeated use of their components and materials when their life ended.

While craft (or, as I like to call it, 'patient') work would be encouraged, this would be no retreat to craft or cottage economies. Technology would continue to be of vital importance. Digital delivery of goods and services would become even more preferable to physical delivery than it is at present. Efficient logistical systems could reduce the cost and carbon footprint of those material goods which had to be transported.

Innovation and the development and application of new technologies would continue to be a major source of new value for companies. Genetically modified crops, nanotechnology, nuclear and other new sources of power all offer both much potential and much risk. Provided the dangers are fully understood and taken into account – and they are not used to displace traditional sustainable practices – they all offer new ways of helping towards the establishment of sustainable societies.

Education will be another area of special focus. Combined with information technology and communication needs, future societies will have no lack of demand for scientists, technicians and other skilled workers. Raising standards for women, a resource still woefully under-used in many Asian countries, would be a particularly rich area for development.

One of the crucial decisions Asian societies will have to face in the coming decades is what to do about urbanization, and in particular, whether they should be rethinking the current drive towards an ever greater number of ever larger mega-cities.

Most development theorists encourage urbanization, while pointing out that cities must become more efficient in their use of resources. The underlying reasoning is that urban jobs, be they in manufacturing or services, create far more value than rural ones – massively so. The average manufacturing job adds three times as much value as a farming job, and the average services job around five times as much. Therefore, the best thing for development is to have cities with lots of manufacturing and services, leaving as few people in the countryside as possible. The outcome is societies like the United States, where farming accounts for a tiny fraction of work – less than 2 percent of jobs – and an even smaller share of GDP – less than 1 percent. In India, by contrast, agriculture accounts for 17 percent of GDP but more than half of all jobs.[9]

It is not surprising, therefore, that countries see increasing the number of urban jobs as a high priority. No country is doing this faster than China, which has seen the share of its population living in urban areas rise from just a quarter in 1990, to around half now, and forecasts a rise to around 70 percent over the next fifteen to twenty-five years.

But is this really the right way to go? Urbanization makes sense in terms of the Western economic model. But in Asia, where some two billion people still live in the countryside, there have to be huge question marks over such a strategy. Aside from expanding what are already some of the world's most polluted cities, the very notion that what is needed are more manufacturing jobs producing cheap goods for export should itself be questioned.

Cities take a disproportionate amount of the overall resources of any country, sucking in water, power, food and people from their hinterlands. Future gains in efficiency could help lessen their impact, as buildings use less energy and other resources, especially if public transport systems were to displace private cars. There will be urban centres and we will need to make them better. But just accepting that this is the course of development, and concentrating more people in large cities, is counter-productive.

Asian policy makers need to look at alternatives – above all, the dispersed development model, briefly described in Chapter 5. By linking towns and rural districts into integrated networks, development can be spread broadly across a country instead of concentrated in a few mega-cities. Such a model is likely to disperse both resource use and opportunities, creating more equitable and sustainable societies.

Information and communications technology can help here, by linking businesses into larger regional and even international markets where necessary, as can transport systems that promote mobility rather than offering individuals the means to drive private cars. Future energy systems may well be based around such dispersed networks, especially those using agricultural waste for fuel. Also important would be rural banking systems that can deliver credit to small-scale enterprises and farmers of the kind mentioned earlier.

These proposals have the potential to constrain the resource demands of growth while simultaneously dispersing it more broadly. Through measures encouraging greater local production of goods and services, regional development can be re-engineered away from its current emphasis on creating ever bigger urban centres and towards the creation of more small units, towns and townships.

Such solutions look like they could have been applicable in Mongolia, where families must have possibilities for earning a living that extend beyond moving to the outskirts of Ulan Batur. Likewise, in Thailand, the way villages spend funds on developing business aimed at establishing self-sufficiency perhaps just needs better technical support – an internet connection that allows villagers to report how the money is being spent to officials in the nearest regional city. China has been attempting to follow this route with its 'Go West' campaign, aimed at encouraging investment in its poorer central and western regions.

Finance

Finally, an area in special need of attention is finance. As we saw during the global financial crisis, banks that know their governments will bail them out will inevitably take on too much risk. But more important than this, governments must also address finance's role as business's great enabler. This requires setting frameworks governing not just the risk banks take, but what their money is doing.

Financial systems do perform vital functions, but their participants must not be allowed to extend their business beyond these functions unless they can clearly demonstrate that benefits will arise – and not just benefits to the pay packets of bankers. In particular, claims that any new product 'adds value' would have to be closely scrutinized. As became all too clear in 2008, many of the supposed innovations of the previous decade were in fact Ponzi schemes, reliant on huge amounts of leverage to generate returns on deals whose element of risk had been seriously underestimated.

Regulation of bank operations will be constrained by environmental considerations, but they would also benefit from being subject to an explicit ethical framework. The outcome would be financial institutions that looked more like utilities than the machines for greed they made themselves into in the years before the financial crisis. Financial transaction taxes, such as the 'Tobin tax' proposed by American economist James Tobin that would be levied on foreign exchange transactions in order to reduce speculation in global currency markets, might be usefully explored.

The primary task of banks in Asia should be to facilitate business, for which they can rightfully charge a reasonable fee, not to trade on their own account or – worse still – invent products whose main purpose is to create trades or other fee-generating transactions of direct benefit to the banks themselves but of little or no value to their clients.

There would seem to be no *a priori* reason for not compelling financial institutions to be subject to rules governing the environmental impact of their lending and other decisions. The Equator Principles, a set of voluntary standards for assessing environmental impact in project finance, offer a template but one whose rules need both stiffening and to be made legally enforceable. Technology could play a major role in monitoring deals: much as money laundering has been targeted in the post 9-11 world, so environmental 'laundering' should be subject to the same kind of scrutiny.

If bank profits rise to the heights they did in the run up to the financial crisis, there should be major suspicions that this money is coming from unsustainable sources such as sub-prime mortgages and the derivatives built from them. Banks should not be allowed to monitor themselves through voluntary codes of conduct or similar protocols. As we have seen, they are not capable of policing themselves, even when their own interests are at stake.

Thus, while finance can play a major role in addressing the issues of constraint, it cannot be left to operate unhindered; instead governments must determine the framework within which banks and other financial institutions act, and then monitor them closely to ensure compliance. Overall, finance must be regulated like a utility, expected to provide a reliable range of necessary funding and other financial services, and subjected to caps on its profits. Finance's role can only be as a supporting tool; it should never be seen as an alternative to strong policies and regulations on consumption.

Companies, likewise, should not be looked to as a source of solutions. Their preference – until they are compelled to think otherwise – will be for the system that created them. They will look for ways of improving their own short-term interests, regardless of the impact this has on the rest of the world. And that will remain their reason for being until change is forced upon them by governments.

Where possible, governments must find ways of working with companies that are mutually beneficial. But if in doubt, officials should not hesitate to apply rules and licensing practices that clearly specify what behaviour is or is not acceptable. Much work can be done in corporate governance, ensuring that businesses and their lobbying bodies, such as the International Chamber of Commerce, Nippon Keidanren, World Business Council for Sustainable Development and the Palm Oil Industry Roundtable on Sustainability, are transparent and accountable, and are not permitted to confer respectability on unsustainable or socially destructive business practices.

A good share of the responsibility for many people believing that companies have a key role in coming up with solutions for climate change and the other environmental threats facing the planet stems from the media. This is seen at its worst in the lazy approach towards examining the PR-driven green clichés of multinational companies, epitomized by the *Financial Times'* 'Sustainable Banking Awards', a particularly fine example of the superficiality that accompanies most corporate efforts at demonstrating their environmental awareness. Given such trivialization of what is a profoundly serious issue, it is unsurprising that most corporate social responsibility practices are cosmetic. They will remain that way while businesses are self-policing in this area.

Self-regulation via voluntary codes of conduct must be regarded with particular suspicion – there have been too many instances of companies sheltering behind such measures to mask irresponsible practices, as the financial crisis highlighted.

Beyond Western capitalism

For the last two centuries, Western capitalism has regarded itself as the world's most progressive force. It saw the ever-continuing rise in prosperity it delivered as largely stemming from its ability to apply scientific knowledge and technology to the natural world, while its emphasis on democracy and rights allowed it to claim that people were much freer from persecution and more able to protect their own interests than in any preceding societies in world history. The contribution of colonialism to this process of wealth creation was naturally downplayed, and the impact of its activities on the environment largely ignored. That democracy has hindered the development of many poorer countries is one of its aspects that most Western commentators prefer to play down. Thailand's recent experiences come to mind, as do the longer histories of the Philippines and India for much of its post-independence era.

Through the second half of the twentieth century, these archaic notions of racial supremacy fortunately diminished. But replacing them as the pre-eminent explanation of Western wealth were economic ideas, with the role of free markets taking on an ever greater importance. These ideas received their greatest sanction when the West's big ideological rival, the Soviet Union, collapsed, taking with it the last vestiges of communism's claim that it offered a superior way of harnessing nature to produce prosperity and freedom.

The Western model, however, has reached its limits. It may have won the Cold War, but in its place it upped its war on nature. Now the time has come to end that war too. What we must do now is look for new ways of running societies – ones that build on the achievements of Western civilisation instead of trying to emulate it.

For the foreseeable future our societies will be capitalist. Even in China, where state-owned companies have successfully retained control over the economy's most strategic sectors, most decisions on supply, demand and pricing are likely to be broadly set by markets, not government diktat.

But until now, capitalism has had an incentive to treat resources and the natural environment as low-cost or free items. That must no longer be the case. Resources and environmental services must be expensive to the point where companies strive to use as few inputs and ecological services as possible.

Consequently the form of capitalism that will emerge in the coming decades will also have to be very different from the Western model that has dominated since the Second World War. We must strive to establish a constrained form of capitalism – one where the cost of human resource use and its impact on the environment is priced in from the start, not added as an afterthought. This should also be a capitalism that is treated as a means, not an end. No longer will the establishment of markets be the goal societies strive to realize; rather, markets must be used as tools, subject to limitations on their exploitation of materials and other inputs, and barred from expansion when threatening to deplete vital natural assets.

A big claim of market mechanisms is that they are more efficient. We have to accept that in many of the circumstances we are looking at, we simply do not want improved efficiency: we do not want improved efficiency in the felling of forests or exploitation of fisheries; we do not want more fuel-efficient cars if the outcome is more driving, more congestion, more road building and more extraction of oil from ever more remote and ecologically sensitive locations. In Asia, we simply cannot afford this 'efficiency'. However, a lot of the problems 'efficiency' causes can be circumvented by pricing in external factors. Because resources and ecological services have been underpriced in the past, market prices reflected distorted costs. Efficiency with true prices for resources would lead to a search for efficiency in other areas, such as resource productivity.

Capitalism will be reshaped, not replaced. Via markets, it still offers the best machinery for allowing people to choose what they want, encourage innovation, and determine the allocation of goods and pricing according to demand and supply. But it must operate in a framework based around strict resource-management rules – one with constraints on consumption, constructed by pricing in external factors and, where necessary, incorporating curbs or bans on the use of various resources. Determining its form will be the changed incentives it will be subject to.

This means governments must establish frameworks within which companies operate, ensuring that the environmental impact of their operations is included in costs, that everyone has fair access to the resources they need, and that a few are not consuming to the detriment of the many – be that today or over time.

These governments will in most cases have to be stronger and more effective than they are now. As countries now stand, China, perhaps, has the greatest potential for realizing change along the lines described in this book. It looks likely to introduce a nationwide resources tax, and within five years may also have a carbon tax.[10]

But it is not alone. India will need more powerful, confident and less corruptible officials if it is to withstand ever more prevalent business lobbying. But there are signs of change. The refusal in 2010 of its environment ministry to grant UK-based Vedanta Resources permission to mine bauxite in eastern India was a major step in the right direction. Officials cited violations of environmental and human rights laws in their decision. But also important were the growing complaints from middle-class Indians about the way their country's development was being hijacked by industrial interests happy to trample over the rights of local communities. Already, despite still being at a very early stage of development, Indians are starting to wonder about the true cost of their country's growth.

Markets will continue to have a major role. But they are not, and cannot be, the solution to the world's ills. All too often, corporate interests remain steadfast in securing returns for themselves and their owners, whatever the negative environmental and social impact of their activities. Tobacco companies have long exemplified such businesses, but in the coming decades they are likely to be joined by automotive, mining, fossil fuel and fast-food corporations. Markets must be scrutinized and subject to oversight on both their demand and supply sides. They must be prevented from prolonging the status quo and its beneficiaries. The ways in which they shape demand and the techniques they use to meet it must be regulated in ways that only allow environmentally sustainable and socially equitable outcomes.

Optimistic?

In this book's preface, I declared myself an optimist. And I certainly believe the world can forgo the consumption-driven ways that have fuelled growth until now. But the dreams that have been created along the way – that everyone can have it all – will be hard to dispel. I do not foresee the world's rich countries voluntarily opting to end their current lifestyles and put growth into reverse. Even less can I envisage multinational companies willingly embracing restraint and moderation.

But there is a chance of change – from Asia. Already, the region is exploring alternative models. Japan has a tradition of sustainability that it is now taking further. Forests cover some 70 percent of its land, and provide most of its timber. Its agriculture may be highly subsidized, but farming remains part of most landscapes, including many urban locations. Not only do more than five million people continue to secure their food direct from farmers, but much of the country's food remains local, traditional and available in huge variety – witness its more than 150 varieties of rice. Due to high energy costs, Japanese labour remains competitive in both traditional and modern sectors of its economy, and the country continues to have a bias towards the employment of people rather than machines, despite also being a world leader in the construction of industrial robots.

Such a balance is in good part due to its unwritten social contract – that individuals should be taken care of by the group.

Elsewhere, its ecological practices may be weaker. Its fish consumption in particular is unsustainable, and it spends far too much on unnecessary infrastructure and construction projects. But nonetheless it has some foundations from which it can evolve towards the establishment of a sustainable economy, building on both its traditions and circumstances.

South Korea is also looking for a different future – perhaps more aggressively than anywhere else. In 2009, it passed a Low Carbon and Green Growth Act aimed at transforming the heavy industry and manufacturing sectors that dominate its economy. Its goal – set unilaterally – is to keep its 2020 greenhouse gas emissions total to less than its actual 2005 levels.

Several of India's struggles to reconcile the differences between the interests of local communities and companies have already been noted. The last year has seen several other significant measures. In late 2009, India announced that it had targeted a reduction in national energy intensity of 25 percent by 2020. At the start of 2010, its prime minister, Manmohan Singh, established a twenty-six-member expert group charged with developing a low-carbon growth strategy for the country. The group's chairperson, Kirit Parikh, singled out some familiar areas for focus, among them solar technology and bio-fuels. Interestingly, he also threw the net rather wider – other issues he sees as crucial are rainwater harvesting and watershed development, an employment law introduced in 2005 that guarantees a hundred days of work each year for all rural adults, and efforts to achieve 100 percent literacy rates and school attendance.

Other countries are also finding their own new ways. Indonesia's agreement with Norway to halt the felling of tropical forest cited in the previous chapter points to the bargaining power that resource-rich countries can bring to bear in not exploiting their resources. In Vietnam, plans to mine bauxite in the Central Highlands, the region where more than three-quarters of the country's coffee is grown, have run into opposition from scientists and an increasingly vocal environmental lobby.[11]

For more than a decade, Bangladesh's New Agricultural Movement has been advocating pesticide-free farming that both draws on and attempts to enhance traditional techniques. Women are particularly important as the guardians of seeds and knowledge about them. Advocating biodiversity and the planting of multiple crops rather than monocultures, the movement has already attracted more than 75,000 households.[12]

And of course there is China, simultaneously growing its economy at a phenomenal rate while announcing hugely ambitious environmental targets. It is home to perhaps the most exciting resource-management projects in Asia – but also some of the most frightening schemes, be they in industry, dam construction or the encouragement of consumption in its leading cities.

The countries of Asia must now take their own paths, irrespective of what the West does, and to a large extent irrespective of each other. The good news is that awareness of the need for national-level action is rising. But the key challenge, more important than any other, will be ensuring that governments get their priorities right. Leadership will be important for this, especially from leaders willing to stand and up say that consumption-driven growth is not the answer; that the top priority is making resource management and protection the centre of all policy making, not promoting development blindly through a reliance on market capitalism.

In relations between countries within Asia and between Asian countries and other parts of the world, particularly the rich countries, governments will have to take a more independent line than they have been used to. The destinies of their countries will lie in their hands, far more so than the advocates (and many of the opponents) of globalization and the so-called 'borderless' world maintained. Countries can set their own rules on resource use.

International institutions such as World Bank, International Monetary Fund and World Trade Organization must be treated with the respect they deserve – which is to say, acknowledged as possible sources of expertise but not as bodies with any right to exercise control over sovereign governments in the setting of economic and other policies. No longer should they be allowed to advance market-driven solutions at the expense of working with local governments and populations in identifying appropriate, more domestically shaped schemes.

If they can take development in the direction envisaged by this book, then they can create new forms of society, very different from those of today's rich or developing world. Asians can engage the world on these issues. They have the means. They have the tools. And increasingly they have the ideas. They have an opportunity to harness development in ways that can meet their needs and desires and produce a global environment that is worth living in.

AFTERWORD

As I mulled over the ideas of this book, I found myself repeatedly asking what I hoped its publication might achieve. Identifying this took some soul searching. Given my rather varied background and career, and the intellectual freedom I am now privileged to enjoy, I felt under something of an obligation to share my thoughts. And, while not wanting to overestimate my ability to influence, nor did I feel any compulsion to mask my strong conviction that the issues under discussion are of crucial importance. (Otherwise why bother to write, and in so doing risk opening myself to ridicule by sharing my thoughts with the world, given the inherently controversial nature of the topic?)

Eventually I decided my hopes for this book centred on the different people who might read it – and that there would be many of them. Not because I am looking to get rich (although I hope that my publisher is rewarded for his faith in this first-time author), but because it is crucial that as many people as possible start thinking about its issues.

Much of what is currently being discussed in terms of Asia's future, capitalism and the resource and environmental challenge we face is steeped in an inability to move beyond a very tired form of conventional wisdom. This is nowhere more visible than in the widespread refusal to accept the limits nature places on what people can do. Even the most magical spells of that twin-headed god, finance and technology, will not allow us to overcome these planetary constraints.

It is because of these limits that we must challenge the widespread notion that the billions of people in Asia should aspire to an American way of life. Such a future is impossible; attempting to realize it would be catastrophic.

In addressing these issues, I do not claim to have all the answers, nor do I suggest that I have covered all the interconnected issues. This is a work in progress, and I hope much smarter minds than mine will be emboldened to take it further. But I do hope that critics, before they pick on the inevitable weaknesses or contradictions they are sure to find, ask whether the questions this book poses about consumption-led capitalism, resource constraints and the environmental impact of human activity can be answered by adopting 'green' technology, fine-tuning markets and the dream of a carbon-neutral world.

I also hope that we can move beyond the shallow responses to these challenges that are typically heard, particularly at business forums which purportedly seek to address these very issues. I hope we can hear more discussion about the constraints that should be applied to consumption and fewer arguments about hypothetical limits on individual freedoms, whether we should be applying more draconian policies in managing our economy and the possibility of banning various egregious forms of consumption.

I hope business and its cheerleaders will not try to trivialize the issues raised by this book in efforts to defend their short-term agendas. As the book explains, these issues are at the core of where Asia goes in the twenty-first century; if governments do opt to put resource management at the centre of their policy-making agendas, the reaction of business will be critical to its success or otherwise.

These are issues which should be discussed by the broadest possible range of people – far beyond the elite discussions held on the pages of the *Financial Times* and *International Herald Tribune*, in the *Economist* or on the BBC, at Davos or the Aspen Institute.

Strong and able governments will be the key force navigating Asia through the twenty-first century. But setting the direction will be policy makers, guided, I hope, by new ideas and sources of knowledge. The first step towards such new thinking will be to explore the implications of Asia's current development trajectory, and ask whether a radical shift in course is not the logical outcome.

Academia has an important role to play in these discussions. The long-established practice of seeking recognition by following Western thought in economics, development theory, public policy and foreign policy needs to be re-examined if we are to find new ideas for Asia's coming decades. If we are to reshape the future, Asian academic institutions must discover their own voice. To do so, they will need adequate local support and funding.

Scientists, I hope, will take note of the call in the book for governments to give science pride of place over economics in planning. Certainly scientists should be encouraged to become more assertive and engaged politically, thereby helping to produce a more responsible capitalism.

A very special hope is that the Asian media will give it attention so that politicians, business leaders, academics and young professionals will read it and start to be part of a process of re-evaluating the direction of economic development. Thus I have another hope – that the book will be translated into all major Asian languages as recognition that one cannot speak only to those educated in English.

And finally, at the level of regional cooperation, I hope regional talking shops such as China's Boao Forum or Asean's Regional Forum will take up some of the themes in this book – regardless of the tensions and confusion that may result.

NOTES

Preface

1. Thomas L. Friedman, 'Off to the Races', *New York Times*, December 9, 2009; available at http://www.nytimes.com/2009/12/20/opinion/20friedman.html (accessed March 3, 2010).

2. For more on the Coral Triangle, a region that embraces some of Asia's most spectacular land and seascapes, see The Nature Conservancy, 'Coral Triangle Center'; available at http://www.coraltrianglecenter.org (accessed August 27, 2010).

Introduction

1. See Gov.cn, 'Full text of Chinese Premier Wen Jiabao's speech at 2009 Summer Davos in Dalian', September 11, 2009: available at http://www.gov.cn/english/2009-09/11/content_1414917.htm (accessed August 12, 2010).

2. Anoop Singh, 'China's growth depends on boosting household income and persuading people to spend more', *South China Morning Post*, March 15, 2010.

3. John Grimond, 'For want of a drink: A special report on water', *The Economist*, May 20, 2010.

4. J.R. McNeill, *Something New Under the Sun: An Environmental History of the Twentieth-Century World*, Norton, New York, 2000, page 357.

5. For a concise outline of his ideas, see Bjørn Lomborg, 'Technology, Not Talks Will Save the Planet', *Finance and Development*, December 2009; available at http://www.imf.org/external/pubs/ft/fandd/2009/12/lomborg. htm (accessed August 30, 2010).

6. John Gray, 'We simply do not know!', *London Review of Books*, Volume 13, Number 22, pages 13–14; available at http://www.lrb.co.uk/v31/n22/ john-gray/we-simply-do-not-know (accessed June 29, 2010).

7. World Bank, 'World Databank', http://data.worldbank.org/ (accessed August 11, 2010).

8. Cited at 'Memorable quotes for Wall Street (1987)', at http://www. imdb.com/title/tt0094291/quotes (accessed August 30, 2010).

9. Paul Krugman's ideas are laid out in crystal-clear prose in 'Building a Green Economy', *New York Times*, April 5, 2010, available at http://www.nytimes.com/2010/04/11/magazine/11Economy-t. html?sq=krugman%20green%20economics&st=cse&scp=1&pagewante d=all (accessed August 18, 2010).

10. Known technically as an environmental Kuznets curve, after the similar curve postulated by Russian-American economist Simon Kuznets, suggesting that income inequality would rise in the early stages of a country's development then decline after a certain level of prosperity was reached.

11. For a discussion of the environmental Kuznets curve, including how governments can accelerate the implementation of pollution controls, see Susmita Dasgupta, Benoit Laplante, Hua Wang and David Wheeler, 'Confronting the Environmental Kuznets Curve', *Journal of Economic Perspectives*, Volume 16, Number 1, Winter 2002, pages 147–168; available at http://citeseerx.ist.psu.edu/viewdoc/summary?doi=10.1.1.127.3264 (accessed August 12, 2010).

12. A United Nations study in 2006 suggested that cattle-rearing generated 18 percent of greenhouse gases measured by carbon dioxide equivalent, while global transportation was responsible for 13 percent. See Food and Agriculture Organization of the United Nations, 'Livestock a major threat to environment', November 29, 2006, available at http://www.fao.org/newsroom/en/news/2006/1000448/index.html (accessed August 30, 2010).

13. James Lovelock sees severe global warming as a given, leading to the likely shrinkage of the world population to just one billion within a century or so; see his *The Vanishing Face of Gaia: A Final Warning*, Allen Lane, London 2009. James Hansen envisages an even worse future – a 'runaway' greenhouse effect that leaves Earth as hot as Venus, and so lifeless; see his *Storms of My Grandchildren: The Truth About the Coming Climate Catastrophe and Our Last Chance to Save Humanity*, Bloomsbury, New York, 2009.

14. In his most recent book (*Common Wealth: Economics For a Crowded Planet*, Penguin, New York, 2008, pages 220-221), Jeffrey Sachs proposes six public interventions of great importance:

- Help for the destitute
- Provision of key infrastructure
- Sound business environment
- Provision of social insurance
- Promotion and dissemination of modern science and technology
- A proper stewardship of the natural environment

What I find incomprehensible is the placement of stewardship of the environment as the final item. As with many commentators, caring for the environment has become something that must be acknowledged, but essentially as an afterthought. As I say in the text, unless the environment is prioritized, there will be little point in attempting to realize the other five of Sachs' proposed interventions.

Chapter 1

1. ThePoultrySite.com, 'Global Poultry Trends 2010', available at http://www.thepoultrysite.com/articles/1751/global-poultry-trends-rising-human-population-and-per-capita-consumption-in-asia-boost-total-chicken-demand (accessed September 3, 2010); Elizabeth Kolbert, 'Flesh of Your Flesh: Should you eat meat?, *New Yorker*, November 9, 2009; available at http://www.newyorker.com/arts/critics/books/2009/11/09/091109crbo_books_kolbert (accessed September 3, 2010).

2. Jeffrey D. Sachs, *Common Weatlh: Economics for a Crowded Planet*, Penguin, New York, 2008, page 23.

3. Basic maths generates these numbers. Annual average growth of 4.25 percent increases economic output 6.5 times between 2005 and 2050; reducing this to 2.75 percent for the following fifty years has an output twenty-five times that of 2005 in 2100.

4. Lester Brown, *Plan B 4.0: Mobilizing to Save Civilization*, Norton, New York, 2009, page 14.

5. *Water: A Shared Responsibility, The United Nations World Water Development Report 2*, UNESCO/Berghahn Books, Paris/New York, 2006, pages 132–3.

6. *Water: A Shared Responsibility, The United Nations World Water Development Report 2*, UNESCO/Berghahn Books, Paris/New York, 2006, page 134.

7. Rainforest information, 'Indonesia', available at http://rainforest.mongabay.com/20indonesia.htm (accessed September 30, 2010).

8. World Bank, *World Development Report 2010, Development and Climate Change*, page 363.

9. Intergovernmental Panel on Climate Change (IPCC), *Fourth Assessment Report, Climate Change 2007: Working Group II: Impacts, Adaption and Vulnerability*, Section 10.4.1, 'Agriculture and food security', available at http://www.ipcc.ch/publications_and_data/ar4/wg2/en/ch10s10-4-1.

html (accessed August 16, 2010).

10. Graham Turner, 'A Comparison of the *Limits to Growth* with Thirty Years of Reality', Socio-Economics and the Environment in Discussion CSIRO Working Paper Series, June 2008, available at http://ideas.repec.org/p/cse/wpaper/2008-09.html (accessed June 15, 2010).

11. Argonne National Laboratory, 'Projection of Chinese Motor Vehicle Growth, Oil Demand, and CO_2 Emissions through 2050', 2006, available at http://www.ipd.anl.gov/anlpubs/2006/12/58260.pdf (accessed August 31, 2010).

12. See Kevin Rafferty, 'China oil shock to shake the world', *South China Morning Post*, August 31, 2010, available at http://www.scmp.com/portal/site/SCMP/menuitem.2af62ecb329d3d7733492d9253a0a0a0/?vgnextoid=ff27270fd43ca210VgnVCM100000360a0a0aRCRD&ss=Analysis&s=Business (accessed September 1, 2010).

13. 'Ghosn – sees global car numbers up sharply by 2050', Reuters, May 30, 2008, available at http://www.reuters.com/article/idUSL3090613120080530 (accessed September 6, 2010).

14. The report, *Our Common Future*, is available at http://www.un-documents.net/wced-ocf.htm (accessed August 31, 2010). The definition of sustainable development is in Chapter 2, at http://www.un-documents.net/ocf-02.htm (accessed August 31, 2010).

15. For a longer, more technical discussion of the possibility of poor country subsidization of rich country consumption, see Kenneth Arrow, Partha Dasgupta, Lawrence Goulder, Gretchen Daily, Paul Ehrlich, Geoffrey Heal, Simon Levin, Karl-Göran Mäler, Stephen Schneider, David Starrett and Brian Walker, 'Are We Consuming Too Much?', September 2003, available at http://www.econ.cam.ac.uk/faculty/dasgupta/toomuch.pdf, page 25 (accessed July 14, 2010).

16. See the work of Neil Englehart cited in David Shearman and Joseph Wayne Smith, *The Climate Change Challenge and the Failure of Democracy*, Praeger, Westport Connecticut, 2007, page 70.

17. Joseph Stiglitz *Freefall*, Norton, New York, 2010 pages 288–9.

18. Chinese obesity statistics from http://www.urbanatomy.com/index. php/i-ahearts-shanghai/features/2722-dieting-fat-china-special-report; Indian ones from Imprimis Knowledge Series III, Fact Sheet: Obesity in India, page 3, available at http://www.imprimispr.com/whitepaper/ White%20paper-obesity.pdf (accessed October 25, 2010).

19. Food Industry India, 'Meat and poultry sector in India – pink revolution possible', May 20, 2010; available at http://www. foodindustryindia.com:9080/newfood/detailnews.jsp?n=Meat%20 and%20poultry%20sector%20in%20India%20%E2%80%93%20 pink%20revolution%20possible&id=780 (accessed August 31, 2010).

Chapter 2

1. Amory B. Lovins and L. Hunter Lovins, *Natural Capitalism: The Next Industrial Revolution*, Earthscan, London, 1999; and Jonathon Porritt, *Capitalism as if the World Matters* (revised edition), Earthscan, London, 2007.

2. Paul Krugman, 'Building a Green Economy', *New York Times*, April 5, 2010, available at http://www.nytimes.com/2010/04/11/ magazine/11Economy-t.html?sq=krugman%20green%20economics&st =cse&scp=1&pagewanted=all (accessed August 18, 2010).

3. Thomas L. Friedman, *Hot, Flat, and Crowded: Why We Need a Green Revolution – and How It Can Renew America*, Farrar, Strauss and Giroux, New York, 2008. The quotation is from Thomas L. Friedman, 'Off to the Races,' *New York Times*, December 19, 2009, available at http://www. nytimes.com/2009/12/20/opinion/20friedman.html (accessed June 10, 2010).

4. Thomas L. Friedman, *Hot, Flat, and Crowded*, Farrar, Strauss and Giroux, New York, 2008.

5. Joseph Stiglitz, 'The Non-Existent Hand', *London Review of Books*, Volume 32, Number 8, April 22, 2010, pages 17–18; available at http://

www.lrb.co.uk/v32/n08/joseph-stiglitz/the-non-existent-hand (accessed June 10, 2010).

6. Of course, this is a simplification – there are companies and countries which shrink or grow very slowly. But in the case of companies, most of these go out of business, usually quite fast; in the case of countries, almost all are regarded as failed states, and certainly not as models for emulation.

7. J.R. McNeill, *Something New Under the Sun: An Environmental History of the Twentieth-Century World*, Norton, New York, 2000, pages 310–1.

8. For a discussion of why mining can only be made sustainable by redefining what 'sustainable' means, see Stuart Kirsch, 'Sustainable mining', *Dialectical Anthropology*, Volume 34, Number 1, August 2009, pages 87–93; available at http://www.springerlink.com/content/ju3q638v453q7vn8/ (accessed August 18, 2010).

9. See S. Dewi, N. Khasanah, S. Rahayu, A. Ekadinata and M van Noordwijk, 'Carbon Footprint of Indonesian Palm Oil Production: a Pilot Study', World Agroforestry Centre – ICRAF, SEA Regional Office, Bogor, Indonesia, 2009, cited in *Up for Grabs: Deforestation and Exploitation in Papua's Plantations Boom*, Environmental Investigation Agency, London, 2009, page 4.

10. United Nations Environment Program, 'Towards Sustainable Production and Use of Resources: Assessing Biofuels', 2009, cited in *Up for Grabs: Deforestation and Exploitation in Papua's Plantations Boom*, Environmental Investigation Agency, London, 2009, page 4.

11. 'Over and over, studies of mergers and acquisitions show that deals fail to create shareholder value. One recent survey says that more than 70 percent of acquisitions fail; another, 61 percent. A third study reports that 89 percent of acquired businesses actually lose market share', Kate Sullivan, 'Secrets of the M&A Masters', *CFO Magazine*, September 1, 2004, available at http://www.cfo.com/article.cfm/4315552?f=RequiredReading (accessed August 17, 2010).

12. See Kathrin Hille, Geoff Dyer and Fiona Harvey, 'UN halts funds to China wind farms', *Financial Times*, December 1, 2009, available at http://www.ft.com/cms/s/0/128a52de-deaf-11de-adff-00144feab49a.html?nclick_check=1, (accessed August 17, 2010).

13. Justin Lahart, Patrick Barta and Andrew Batson, 'New Limits to Growth Revive Malthusian Fears', *Wall Street Journal*, March 24, 2008, available at http://online.wsj.com/article/SB120613138379155707.html (accessed August 18, 2010).

14. Jeffrey Sachs, *Common Wealth: Economics for a Crowded Planet*, Penguin, New York, 2008, page 57. Italics in the original.

15. The impact of the chainsaw is drawn from J.R. McNeill, *Something New Under the Sun: An Environmental History of the Twentieth-Century World*, Norton, New York, 2000, pages 307–8.

16. Tim Jackson, *Prosperity without Growth: Economics for a Finite Planet*, Earthscan, London and Sterling, Virginia, 2009, pages 79–80.

Chapter 3

1. This chapter owes a sizeable debt to the ideas of Kenneth Arrow, Partha Dasgupta, Lawrence Goulder, Gretchen Daily, Paul Ehrlich, Geoffrey Heal, Simon Levin, Karl-Göran Mäler, Stephen Schneider, David Starrett and Brian Walker expressed in 'Are We Consuming Too Much?', September 2003, available at http://www.econ.cam.ac.uk/faculty/dasgupta/toomuch.pdf (accessed July 14, 2010).

2. Quoted in Mike Hulme, *Why We Disagree About Climate Change: Understanding Controversy, Inaction and Opportunity*, Cambridge University Press, Cambridge, 2009, pages 130–1.

3. Paul Krugman, 'Building a Green Economy', *New York Times*, April 5, 2010.

4. Jeffrey Sachs, *Common Wealth: Economics for a Crowded Planet*, Penguin, New York, 2008, page 40.

5. Tim Jackson's *Prosperity Without Growth: Economics for a Finite Planet*, Earthscan, London, 2009, is a good example of the genre, exploring many ideas of relevance to the United Kingdom, where he is based, and other developed countries. It has little to say about the predicaments facing Asia and other parts of the world.

6. My thoughts on risk minimization draw heavily on the ideas of Vaclav Smil, a professor at the University of Manitoba's environment faculty, and in particular his *Global Catastrophes and Trends: The Next Fifty Years*, MIT Press, Cambridge, 2008, pages 238–243.

7. Natural capital is a necessarily vague term covering the world's stock of natural goods and systems. It includes tangible things such as minerals, plants and animals, but can be extended to everything from the services nature provides – such as producing oxygen – to intangibles such as landscapes and views. For a book built around the idea of natural capital, see Paul Hawken, Amory B. Lovins and L. Hunter Lovins, *Natural Capitalism: The Next Industrial Revolution*, Earthscan, London, 1999.

8. Here I am in total agreement with Jeffrey Sachs, who proposes essentially identical ideas. As I mention elsewhere in this book, my disagreement with Sachs is over his failure to address the consumption issues raised by those in both the developed and developing world who are not poor.

9. Eric Randolph, 'Maoist Insurgency Trips Up Rising India', YaleGlobal, July 29, 2010, available at http://yaleglobal.yale.edu/content/maoist-insurgency-trips-rising-india (accessed September 8, 2010).

10. As the authors of 'Are We Consuming Too Much?' note, 'A small but growing body of empirical work suggests that a person's sense of well-being is based not only on her own level (and composition) of consumption but also on the level (and composition) of her consumption relative to the level (and composition) of her "reference group." A given individual may suffer a loss of well being when others' consumption rises, since that person's relative consumption now falls. This can be viewed as another example of an externality. Such interdependence in consumption can compel

individuals to work harder and consume more in order to keep up with the neighbors. This is individually rational, but collectively sub-optimal. Under these circumstances, public policies to discourage consumption (including a general consumption tax) could raise individual well-being.' Keith Arrow et al, 'Are We Consuming Too Much?', op cit, page 13.

11. See 'Has TV changed Bhutan?', BBC News, June 17, 2004, available at http://news.bbc.co.uk/2/hi/entertainment/3812275.stm (accessed September 8, 2010).

Chapter 4

1. World Bank, *World Development Report 2010, Development and Climate Change*, page 332.

2. Vandana Shiva, *Soil, Not Oil: Climate Change, Peak Oil and Food Insecurity*, Zed, London, 2008.

3. A point made by John Gray in *False Dawn: The Delusions of Global Capitalism*, Granta, London, 1998 (updated edition with a new foreword, 2009).

4. World Bank, op cit, page 330. *The Economist* sees things similarly: 'the threat of global warming is an obvious example of how government intervention is needed to deter people from overheating the world', 'Leviathan stirs again', *The Economist*, January 21, 2010.

5. William Easterly, *The White Man's Burden: Why the West's Efforts to Aid the Rest Have Done So Much Ill and So Little Good*, Oxford University Press, Oxford and New York, 2006, pages 82–83.

6. Hernando de Soto, *The Mystery of Capital: Why Capitalism Triumphs in the West and Fails Everywhere Else*, Basic Books, New York, 2000.

7. Or, as John Gray pithily labels the Singaporean version, 'guided capitalism under a rule of law', *False Dawn: The Delusions of Global Capitalism*, Granta, London, 1998 (updated edition with a new foreword, 2009), page 190.

8. Peter Burnell, 'Climate Change and Democratization: a Complex Relationship?', Policy Paper, Heinrich Boll Stiftung, Berlin, November 2009, page 37.

9. David Stanway, 'Bitter winter puts Mongolia in bind over mining', Reuters, February 22, 2010, available at http://www.reuters.com/ article/idUSTRE61L00A20100222 (accessed September 9, 2010); Tania Branigan, 'Mongolia: How the winter of "white death" devastated nomads' way of life', *The Guardian*, July 20, 2010, available at http://www. guardian.co.uk/world/2010/jul/20/mongolia-nomads-livestock-winter- poverty (accessed September 9, 2010).

10. For a discussion of how Singapore has frequently introduced economically efficient but politically unpopular policies without the government's popularity at the polls suffering, see Bryan Caplan, 'Singapore's Political Economy: Two Paradoxes', *Ethos*, Issue 6, July 2009, pages 65–72; available at http://www.cscollege.gov.sg/cgl/pub_ethos_9m1. htm#top (accessed July 20, 2010).

Chapter 5

1. Kenneth Arrow, Partha Dasgupta, Lawrence Goulder, Gretchen Daily, Paul Ehrlich, Geoffrey Heal, Simon Levin, Karl-Göran Mäler, Stephen Schneider, David Starrett and Brian Walker expressed in 'Are We Consuming Too Much?', September 2003, page 14; available at: http:// www.econ.cam.ac.uk/faculty/dasgupta/toomuch.pdf (accessed July 14, 2010).

2. See Bob Inglis and Arthur B. Laffer, 'An Emissions Plan Conservatives Could Warm To,' *New York Times*, December 27, 2008, available at http:// www.nytimes.com/2008/12/28/opinion/28inglis.html (accessed August 23, 2010).

3. For further discussion of capitalism's obsession with labour productivity and the benefits of a switch to emphasizing resource productivity, see L. Hunter Lovins, 'Rethinking Production', in The Worldwatch Institute,

2008 State of the World: Innovations for a Sustainable Economy, Norton, New York, 2008, pages 38-40.

4. Walter R. Stahel, *The Performance Economy*, second edition, Palgrave Macmillan, Basingstoke, 2010.

5. See Susan Harper, 'Walter Stahel on Sustainability Solutions', December 20, 2008, available at http://environmentalism.suite101.com/article.cfm/walter_stahel_on_sustainability_solutions (accessed August 23, 2010).

6. Tim Jackson, *Prosperity without Growth: Economics for a Finite Planet*, Earthscan, London and Sterling, Virginia, 2009, page 136.

7. Walter R. Stahel, 'Sustainable Development and Strategic Thinking', *Chinese Journal of Population, Resources and Environment*, Volume 5, Number 4, 2007.

8. The original and a translation of the law is available at http://www.chinaenvironmentallaw.com/wp-content/uploads/2008/09/circular-economy-law-cn-en-final.pdf (accessed August 23, 2010). For a discussion of the law, see Indigo Development, 'China seeks to develop a 'Circular Economy (CE)', Update 09, available at http://www.indigodev.com/Circular1.html#Update (accessed August 23, 2010).

9. For a discussion of China's resource efficiency goals, see Indigo Development, 'China seeks to develop a 'Circular Economy (CE), http://www.indigodev.com/Circular1.html#Update (accessed August 23, 2010).

10. See 'Asia faces food shortage by 2050 without water reform', Physorg.com, August 17, 2009, available at http://www.physorg.com/news169737873.html (accessed August 20, 2010).

11. John Grimond, 'For want of a drink: A special report on water', *The Economist*, May 22, 2010.

12. Kevin Brown, 'The Asian century calls for a rethink on growth', *Financial Times*, June 30, 2010, available at http://www.ft.com/cms/s/0/34701e9e-847a-11df-9cbb-00144feabdc0.html (accessed July 14, 2010).

13. John Grimond, 'For want of a drink: A special report on water', *The Economist*, May 22, 2010

14. Lester Brown, *Plan B 4.0: Mobilizing to Save Civilization*, Norton, New York, 2009, page 15.

15. Vaclav Smil, *Global Catastrophes and Trends: The Next Fifty Years*, MIT Press, Cambridge, 2008, page 235.

16. Jeffrey Sachs, *Common Wealth : Economics for a Crowded Planet*, *Penguin, New York, 2008,*, page 52

Chapter 6

1. See 'Anthony Giddens: *The politics of climate change*', at http://sustainablecities.dk/en/actions/interviews/anthony-giddens-the-politics-of-climate-change-0 (accessed July 30, 2010), and *The Politics of Climate Change*, Polity Press, Cambridge, 2009, cited in Peter Burnell, 'Climate Change and Democratisation: a Complex Relationship?', Policy Paper, Heinrich Boll Stiftung, Berlin, November 2009, page 5.

2. See Peter Burnell, 'Climate Change and Democratisation: a Complex Relationship?', Policy Paper, Heinrich Boll Stiftung, Berlin, November 2009, page 28.

3. As N. Gregory Mankiw, an economist and member of former US president George Bush's Council of Economic Advisers, has noted, 'Convincing China of the virtues of a carbon tax, however, may prove to be the easy part. The first and more difficult step is to convince American voters, and therefore political consultants, that "tax" is not a four-letter word', in 'One Answer to Global Warming: A New Tax', *New York Times*, September 16, 2007, available at http://www.nytimes.com/2007/09/16/business/16view.html?fta=y (accessed March 3, 2010).

4. See Peter Burnell, 'Climate Change and Democratisation: a Complex Relationship?', Policy Paper, Heinrich Boll Stiftung, Berlin, November 2009, pages 24–25.

5. In 2007, China emited 22.3 percent of global carbon dioxide emissions attributable to fossil fuel burning and cement making, the United States was in second place, with 19.9 percent, then India (5.5 percent), Russia (5.2 percent) and Japan (4.3 percent). See the UN's 'Millennium Development Goals Indicators: Carbon dioxide emissions (CO2)' at http://mdgs.un.org/unsd/mdg/SeriesDetail.aspx?srid=749&crid= (accessed July 30, 2010). Brazil is responsible for just under a third of all worldwide carbon dioxide emissions due to deforestation; Indonesia for just over a quarter. See World Bank, World Development Report 2010: Development and Climate Change, World Bank, Washington, 2010, page 363.

6. For a discussion of the agreement, including the hurdles it has to overcome to be successful, see Norman Jiwan, 'Deforestation moratorium is not panacea?', *The Jakarta Post*, July 1, 2010, available at http://www.thejakartapost.com/news/2010/07/01/deforestation-moratorium-not-panacea.html (accessed July 28, 2010).

7. Kenneth Pomeranz, 'The Great Himalayan Watershed: Water Shortages, Mega-Projects and Environmental Politics in China, India, and Southeast Asia', *New Left Review*, 58, July-August 2009, available at http://www.newleftreview.org/?view=2788 (accessed August 2, 2010).

8. Vivienne Walt, 'The Breadbasket of South Korea: Madagascar', *Time*, November 23, 2008, available at http://www.time.com/time/world/article/0,8599,1861145,00.html (accessed September 15, 2010).

9. Joanna Lillis, 'Kazakhstan: China Looking to Lease Land for Agricultural Purposes', Eurasianet.org, February 3, 2010, available at http://www.eurasianet.org/departments/insight/articles/eav020410.shtml (accessed September 15, 2010).

Conclusion

1. See Kevin Brown, 'The Asian century calls for a rethink on growth', *Financial Times*, June 30, 2010, available at http://www.ft.com/cms/ s/0/34701e9e-847a-11df-9cbb-00144feabdc0.html (accessed July 14, 2010).

2. Caroline Fraser, *Rewilding the World: Dispatches from the Conservation Revolution*, Metropolitan, New York, 2009, cited in John Terborgh, 'Why We Must Bring Back the Wolf', *New York Review of Books*, Volume 57, Number 12, July 15, 2010, available at http://www.nybooks.com/articles/ archives/2010/jul/15/why-we-must-bring-back-wolf/ (accessed July 2, 2010).

3. For a discussion of communism's impact on the environment, see J.R. McNeill, *Something New Under the Sun: An Environmental History of the Twentieth-Century World*, Norton, New York, 2000, pages 331–333.

4. Richard H. Thaler and Cass R. Sunstein, *Nudge: Improving Decisions About Health, Wealth, and Happiness* (Revised and Expanded Edition), Penguin, New York, 2009.

5. Do Je-hae, 'Food Waste to Be Slashed by 20%', *Korea Times*, December 30, 2009, available at http://www.koreatimes.co.kr/www/news/ nation/2010/01/117_58233.html (accessed June 13, 2010).

6. See TRAFFIC East Asia and WWF Hong Kong, 'The Hong Kong Trade in Live Reef Fish for Food', no date, available at http://www.traffic. org/species-reports/traffic_species_fish18.pdf (accessed August 3, 2010).

7. Michael Pollan, 'The Food Movement, Rising', *New York Review of Books*, Volume 57, Number 10, June 10, 2010, page 32.

8. See Jyoti Thottam, 'Social Fabric', *Time*, February 22, 2010, available at http://www.time.com/time/printout/0,8816,1963582,00.html (accessed September 15, 2010).

9. For US data, see Carolyn Dimitri, Anne Effland, and Neilson Conklin, 'The 20th Century Transformation of US Agriculture and Farm Policy',

US Department of Agriculture, Electronic Information Bulletin Number 3, June 2005; available at http://www.ers.usda.gov/publications/EIB3/EIB3.htm (accessed August 9, 2010). For Indian data, see Central Intelligence Agency, 'The World Factbook', downloaded from https://www.cia.gov/library/publications/the-world-factbook/geos/in.html#Econ (accessed August 9, 2010).

10. Fu Jing, 'Carbon tax likely, expert forecasts', *China Daily*, May 10, 2010, available at: http://www.chinadaily.com.cn/china/2010-05/10/content_9826546.htm (accessed September 13, 2010).

11. Tran Dinh Thanh Lam, 'Vietnam farmers fall to bauxite bulldozers', *Asia Times Online*, June 2, 2009, available at http://www.atimes.com/atimes/Southeast_Asia/KF02Ae01.html (accessed September 13, 2010); James Hookway, 'Vietnam's Mining Tussle', *The Wall Street Journal*, May 1, 2009, available at http://online.wsj.comonline.wsj.com/article/NA_WSJ_PUB:SB124108600267472569.html (accessed September 13, 2010).

12. Jahangir Alam Jony, 'Nayakrishi Andolon: Recreating Community Biodiversity-based Farming', (undated), available at http://www.grain.org/gd/en/case-studies/cases/doc-pdf/as-full-bangladesh-en.pdf (accessed September 13, 2010).

ACKNOWLEDGEMENTS

This book's origins lie in the countless conversations, debates and arguments I have had with numerous people from my school and university days onwards. Among them are discussions with friends, professionals and strangers in many countries from Africa to the USA, from China to Australia, and from India to Europe.

The ideas in the book have been shaped by far too many to name. They include former teachers, academics, professional colleagues, politicians, business leaders, bankers and activists.

In my current work with the Global Institute for Tomorrow (GIFT), I have had the privilege and opportunity to meet many people living in very demanding situations across Asia. From them, I have also learned a great deal.

I would also like to thank those who have not seen eye to eye with me on many of the book's issues, challenging my views but remaining tolerant and friendly despite our disagreements.

For the support of my colleagues at GIFT, I owe a great deal. They have remained ever patient despite my frequent interruptions to test ideas and thoughts. I would particularly like to thank Feini Tuang for her assistance with the research for this book, and most importantly for also believing.

Those who are close to me and have had the greatest influence on me and my ideas over the years know who they are. I am deeply grateful to them.

A very special thank you goes to Simon Cartledge for helping me with the writing and arguments of this book. He often played that all-important role of stubborn sounding board, thereby helping me to sharpen both my ideas and the language in which they are expressed.

This book would not be possible without the support of several Asian business leaders who took the bold step of supporting the underwriting of it. They have asked to remain anonymous, but I hope others will follow their example and support Asian writers wanting to voice their thoughts.

My book owes a great deal to all these people, though only I can take ownership of the views expressed, the arguments made, the tone used, the errors made and the contradictions inadvertently, but almost certainly, present.

Finally, I would like to thank my publisher, Richard Burton, and his team for their enthusiasm and support from our first conversation onwards – without them, you would not be holding this book in your hands.

INDEX